Singleness~ An Opportunity for Growth and Fulfillment

Edward F. & Gwen Weising

Gospel Publishing House/Springfield, Mo. 65802

02-0901

©1982 by the Gospel Publishing House, Springfield, Missouri 65802. All rights reserved. No part of this book may be reproduced, stored in a retrieval system, or transmitted in any form or by any means, electronic, mechanical, photocopy, recording, or otherwise, without prior written permission of the copyright owner, except brief quotations used in connection with reviews in magazines or newspapers.

Library of Congress Catalog Card Number 82-80197
International Standard Book Number 0-88243-901-4
Printed in the United States of America

A teacher's guide for individual or group study with this book is available from the Gospel Publishing House.

Contents

1 An Explosion of Singles 4
2 Singles—Who Are They? 12
3 The Needs of Singles 22
4 The Opportunities of Singleness—Relationships 33
5 The Opportunities of Singleness—Personal Growth 42
6 The Opportunities of Singleness—Discovering Sexuality 51
7 Singles in Crisis—Divorce 62
8 Singles in Crisis—Widowed 73
9 Singles in Crisis—The Single Parent 83
10 The Church and Singles—Establishing a Singles Ministry 92
11 The Church and Singles—Expanding the Singles Ministry 101
12 The Church and Singles—Expanding Through Singles Conferences 112
13 Single Power 121

1

An Explosion of Singles

Fifty-two million people in the United States are single, and the number is growing continually. The figure has steadily increased through the '60s and '70s, and is still rising in the '80s.

The increase of the single population is not a passing fad or a short-term happening. It has all the earmarks of becoming a set pattern. Some have said that by the year 2000 perhaps half the population of the United States may be single. That remains to be seen, but today the single population constitutes a great mass of people for whom Christ died. *What a tremendous opportunity for the Church!*

The world, always looking for ways to make more money, has risen to the occasion. Singles resorts, restaurants, apartments, and condominiums are springing up everywhere. Singles newspapers, nightclubs, and organizations abound. Singles desirous of a more year-round association can enroll in singles clubs. The advertising for one singles condominium boasted of it as "a sort of sexual supermarket chockful of glittering new goodies to help obliterate painful old memories."

The human fallout from all of this is profuse.

An article in *U.S. News and World Report* commented: "No matter how plush their homes, single people still face one common problem—loneliness." ("Rise of the Singles—40 Million Free Spenders," *U.S. News and World Report* [October 7, 1974]:55.)

If the single is physically unattractive or socially inept, he or she faces a never-ending round of rejection. The whole singles scene can begin to look very empty, very contrived.

The Opportunity

The Church has never had a better opportunity for teaching and evangelization than that provided by the expanding singles population. However, historically our churches have emphasized family and children to the extent of almost totally excluding consideration for the single adult.

Steve Johnson, in the *Seattle Post-Intelligencer,* said: "For singles new to Seattle, it is more hell than heaven as they try to find their niche in the Northwest's couple-oriented society where little recognition is given to their special needs."

Frank Schneider, who has worked for many years among singles, related the following:

"The fact that adult singles in some cases have been considered misfits was underscored not long ago when someone asked how we were doing with the 'unclaimed blessings.' At one time we would probably have laughed, but now we felt a stab of pain because we have made one of the greatest discoveries of a lifetime. For the first time in years of Christian service, we were aware of an affluence of intelligent, capable, loyal, energetic, talented single adults who only wanted someone to care enough to recognize they exist. Some lonely, some deeply hurt, others very self-sufficient and quite in control, but all desiring fellowship in a Christian atmosphere where they can feel they belong."

Jesus said: "Look on the fields; for they are white already to harvest" (John 4:35). A multitude of singles await us—people who are desperate for acceptance and someone who will care about them. Jesus wants us to reach out to these singles in love, for God desires "all men to be saved, and to come unto the knowledge of the truth" (1 Timothy 2:4).

There is transforming power in loving acceptance. We see it in the life of Zaccheus when Jesus said, "Come down here, I want to go with you to *your* house." We see it in the life of the woman who bathed Jesus' feet with her tears. He allowed her to come into His presence, to touch Him. Others were appalled and did not want to become "contaminated" by her. But Jesus, seeing her heart, which was already ravaged by guilt, showed her forgiveness and loving acceptance. She knew she was forgiven because she was accepted.

Jesus did not condone the sin in the lives of these people. We should never accept sin. But Jesus did accept each person as he was and redeemed him. Jesus said: "As my Father hath sent me, even so send I you" (John 20:21). We are His representatives bringing His redemption to all men, including a vast population of singles who have been crushed by divorce, grief, and rejection.

Reasons for the Increase of Singles

The increase in the singles population is due to a number of reasons. Nine percent of singles are separated, 17 percent are divorced, 44 percent are widowed, and 30 percent have never married.

Divorce

When we speak of a growing singles population, perhaps the first thing that comes to mind is the growing divorce rate.

The divorce rate in this country has increased 700 percent in the last century. In the year 1900, divorce was almost unheard of. Only 0.6 percent of all marriages ended in divorce that year. In postwar 1945, the rate rose to 2 percent. In 1970, just 10 years ago, the rate was still comparatively low—3.4 percent per year. But by 1978 it had risen to a yearly rate of 5.2 percent.

Unfortunately, the percentage rate is still continuing its relentless climb. During the first 6 months of 1979, there were 570,000 divorces in the United States. That is an increase of 2 percent over the previous year.

There was a short space of time (about 2 or 3 years) when it was felt that perhaps the divorce rate was slowing or at least holding steady. If that were ever the case it is no longer true. The present rate means that half the marriages in this country are ending in divorce.

Lionel Tiger, in an article titled "Omnigamy: The New Kinship System," published in *Psychology Today*, said it is astonishing that marriage is still allowed:

> If nearly half of anything else ended so disastrous-

ly, the government would surely ban it immediately. If half the tacos served in restaurants caused dysentery, if half the people learning karate broke their palms, if only 6 percent of people who went on roller coasters damaged their middle ears, the public would be clamoring for action.

Yet the most intimate of disasters—with consequences that may last a lifetime for both adults and children—happens over and over again. (Lionel Tiger, "Omnigamy: The New Kinship System," *Psychology Today* [July 1978]:14.)

In 1969, a California legislature enacted a "No-Fault" Family Law Act. The law does away with the complications of legal entanglements and streamlines divorces. One of the marriage partners may ask for the divorce. He or she does not have to prove the other guilty of adultery, nonsupport, or mental cruelty. The charge may simply be an "irretrievably broken marriage."

Almost every state has adopted some type of no-fault divorce law. Since the enactment of this law, the divorce rate in California has risen 9 percent. In Oregon, it is possible to obtain a divorce by mail if there are no children and no complex financial settlement problems.

Divorce is rampant in our land and is a major contributing factor to the growing singles population.

New Roles for Women

Just a few years ago career choices for women were limited. A few braved the masculine world to become doctors, lawyers, and businesswomen. But more often women settled into traditional roles—teachers, secretaries, waitresses, and nurses. It was more or less expected that all women would and should eventually marry and have children. At that time, these women would quit their jobs, stay home, and raise their children.

When World War II came along, life changed drastically. Women were pressed into all kinds of work that had been traditionally thought of as "men's work." "Rosie the Riveter" typified the new attitude that settled on the American scene. Never again were women to stay at home in the numbers they had before the war.

Next came the feminist movement with more changes in store for American women. Now they became truck drivers, construction workers, fire fighters, and a host of other things traditionally thought to be in man's domain. Not only did they assume new types of work, but they also began to expect equal pay for equal work. Many women are now competing with men for the best money to be made.

With secure jobs and more money available to them, these women are able to support themselves quite comfortably. Some have chosen not to marry at all.

Sixty percent of all singles are women, and half that number are under 30 years of age. Women who have been unhappily married for years, now divorce and reestablish themselves as singles because they are better able to support themselves. In 1978, there were 8 million families supported by women not living with a husband—an increase of 44 percent in 8 years.

Later Marriages

Another reason for the increase in the singles

population is the baby boom. Children who were born between 1947 and 1957 are now in their twenties and thirties. Many of them have chosen not to marry.

Some young people of this time period became disillusioned by the breakups of their parents' marriages and decided to delay, if not postpone indefinitely, the time of their own marriages. This does not necessarily mean that all of these people are living alone. The number of unmarried couples living together has doubled in 8 years.

Singleness, an Acceptable Life-style

A new attitude about single living has begun to emerge. Singleness has gained respectability. In our churches, too, there is a growing number of singles who have not been through the trauma of divorce or widowhood. These are the individuals who have chosen singleness, at least for the present, as God's will for their lives.

Once single life was looked on as a temporary passage to married life, a transition period between college and wedlock. Singles were largely young people who were frantically looking for someone to marry.

There were some divorced people, although not the great number there is today. Widowed people were not thought of as "singles," but simply as "widows" or "widowers."

Today, however, many people are thinking of singleness as a permanent life-style. Each year the single population grows a little older, a little more settled into their patterns, and perhaps just a little more content with their single status.

These singles, the never-married, are looking for acceptance too. Many of them have grown up in the Church. The kind of acceptance they are seeking is that which recognizes them as full-fledged members of the body of Christ. It calls upon them to serve in positions of responsibility and leadership just as married couples do. The Church must realize the valuable resource it has in the lives of these enthusiastic and capable people.

Often singleness carries with it a connotation of not being whole or of being somewhat immature, even though the single is by all other standards classified as an adult. But is there an instant maturity that comes with marriage? Is a married person more whole than a single person? Before you answer, remember that Jesus was single; as were Paul and many other great leaders in the Church throughout the centuries.

The Bible states that singles have great potential for Christian service (1 Corinthians 7); sometimes even more than married persons have.

* * * * *

Out of the divorces; the disillusionment with marriage; widowhood; the singles bars, clubs, apartments, and condominiums, comes a torrent of need, and it is flowing right past the door of our churches. But with the pain, loneliness, and need, there is also boundless talent and creativity in that flood of singles. The Church can help and it can also be helped. It can give and it can receive; it can pour out and it can drink in. The opportunity is there. *What will we do?*

2

Singles—Who Are They?

Singles can be classified in a number of ways. The word *single* includes those who have always been single; the widowed, divorced, or separated; and in some cases, the physically handicapped. These people have in the past been labeled with some rather unkind names. They have been called "unclaimed blessings," "old maids," "old bachelors," "spinsters," and a host of other disparaging names.

All of life is a gift from God. Marriage is a gift, but so is singleness. Read what Paul says in 1 Corinthians 7:7,8. Singleness is a special gift for special people. We say we believe every person, single or otherwise, is important. We say God has a plan and a purpose for each life. If that is true, He simply cannot have "unclaimed blessings" or "leftovers."

Some singles have been through great trauma and suffering. Some never have. Some are very capable, well-adjusted individuals who prefer singleness. All of them need a firsthand, personal encounter with Jesus Christ.

Always Single

Sharon is one of the most attractive young

women you may ever meet. She is tall and has shining black hair. Her black eyes sparkle with intelligence, fun, and merriment.

Sharon is single. Why? "Well," she says, "some people say I'm too picky. But I don't really think so. I would like to be married someday—but not just to be married. If a person wants to be married and isn't concerned that it is the right person, she can be married. That isn't too hard to do. But I want it to be right, and I'll wait until it is."

Sharon is one of a growing number of people who are single mainly because they have chosen, at least for a time, to be single.

Some are pursuing careers that would be slowed or stopped altogether by a marriage, home, and children. Others have careers that demand 12 to 14 hours of work every day and leave little time for developing the kind of relationship that leads to marriage.

Many people simply have not yet met a person with whom they would like to spend their entire lives. Some of these individuals are unhappy as they continue their search, but others realize they can't wait until a future "by-and-by" time to have a fulfilled, happy life. These people have set about making a place for themselves—a home, a career, a future.

We know very few single people who do not want to be married someday. But more and more singles are able to accept their single status and get on with the business of living.

There are those individuals who are single because they have renounced marriage in order to serve God on the mission field, or among the disadvantaged of our cities. They realize a home and family would make such a life more complicated and their work more difficult.

There are also children who remain single to care for their aging parents. These people are single because they have made that choice.

It is too costly for us, the Church, to think of the never-married person as somehow different, strange, or incomplete. By having such an attitude, we hinder the single person, causing him to be less effective for God. We need to accept him as he is and incorporate him into our fellowship and body, so he can become all God wants him to be.

Single by Divorce

In the future, we are going to meet more and more people who are divorced. The divorce rate is steadily climbing month by month and year by year.

No longer can the Church put its head in the sand and hope the problem will go away. Rather than going away, we find that divorce is occurring more frequently within the Church itself.

Dennis had been divorced about 2 years when he first came to FOCAS (Fellowship of Christian Adult Singles).* He had been a Christian throughout the 4 years of his marriage and continued to be a Christian when it came to an end. He was one of those who had never considered the possibility of a divorce in his life. He didn't think it could happen to him. But it happened, and he was devastated by it.

---

*Registered servicemark

Immediately after his divorce, he found a small group of Christians, some of them in similar circumstances, who were willing to share in a very open way. The group provided a place where he could feel accepted and share his deep hurts with others. It gave him time to begin to pull his life together.

Part of the reason the marriage didn't work, Dennis feels, is that he had never learned who he was and what true friendship really means.

FOCAS provided a place where he could learn the importance of different levels of friendship. He began to accept himself as he nurtured close friendships. He learned that people can have fun together. Camping trips, volleyball games, retreats, and helping others all became a part of his life. Each event caused him to grow a little more.

Now, several years later, he is the leader of a seminar called "Divorce Recovery." He is helping other newly divorced persons learn how to put their lives back together.

"It doesn't happen all at once," he says. "You have to give yourself time—lots of it."

The divorced person has been something of a problem for the Church. It is not a new problem. Moses had to deal with it in his time. The Pharisees attempted to trap Jesus by asking Him questions regarding divorce. Paul also faced the divorce issue in the Early Church.

Divorce is not what God wants for His children. It falls far short of His ideal—one man for one woman for life—but neither is divorce the unpardonable sin. It is one of the unfortunate things that can happen to some people. Probably no one hates divorce more than the divorced person. He has firsthand experience with the loss that divorce brings.

Most newly divorced people are hurting. What they need most is to be loved and accepted just the way they are. They need someone to talk with who cares about them. They need time to begin to grow in a safe place.

Who is better equipped to provide understanding and acceptance than born-again Christians who are also loved and accepted by Jesus? Who should be better able to listen and care than those who are admonished to show their Christianity by their love? What better, safer place than the Church is there for being sheltered and protected while the gaping wounds heal? We must be willing to provide these helps for the divorced person.

Single by Separation

A sometimes overlooked group of single people is those who are single by separation. Some of these people are living apart from their mates while trying to sort through problems, attitudes, and feelings about their marriages. Some will be reunited with their mates and will continue to live together. Probably that will happen only if they are able to get good counseling and work out the problem areas in their lives.

Separated people are in need of ministry as much as anyone else. They should not be overlooked, but included in a singles ministry.

There are also those who are married but live alone much of the time because their spouses are in military service. These individuals have special needs. They are married, but for long periods of time they are very much alone.

Others are married to a spouse who is involved in a business that takes him or her away from the home for business trips several times each year.

Those single by separation, especially if the separation becomes more or less permanent, may be ready to join a singles group. They have a special problem in that they are single-but-not-single. They have the same needs, frustrations, problems, and time for sharing and serving as other singles, but they are not truly free to pursue the single life-style.

The single-by-separation person should be encouraged to state his position when he joins the group in order to avoid difficult entanglements that would hurt himself or others.

Single by Death

Perhaps the most reluctant group of singles is those who are single because of the death of their marriage partner. Probably most of these people were reasonably happily married. They have not undergone the trauma and problems that often precede divorce.

Suddenly—and it doesn't seem to matter whether or not death was expected—they are alone. A wrenching, tearing sense of loss sets in. The finality of the situation takes a long time to be fully understood.

Immediately upon the death of a spouse, the survivor must deal with financial problems, legal entanglements, funeral details, and a host of other matters.

At first there is great concern and a desire on

the part of friends and the church to care for the widowed person. But within a short time, friends go back to their own lives and the bereaved person is left to fend for himself. It is a very lonely time.

Widowed people, particularly women, suffer a tremendous loss of identity or personhood. They were someone's mate; now they are alone. Once someone cared for them, told them they were loved and needed; now there is no one to say those words.

Perhaps at no other time is the one-flesh concept of marriage so deeply understood as at the death of a marriage partner. The two had grown side by side, becoming more entwined with the years, even to the point of being grafted together in some places. Then one is ripped away from the other. Such tearing leaves the remaining partner shredded, bent, bruised, and torn.

The Bible gives a great deal of instruction about the care of widows and the fatherless. We usually think of the widowed in this case as women. But men are left alone too, and have tremendous needs upon the death of a spouse.

Loren was such a person. He had been married for 10 years and was the father of three daughters when his wife became ill with cancer. Within a short time her condition worsened and she died. To further complicate matters, one of the girls also developed a form of cancer and outlived her mother by little more than a year. In addition, Loren had surgery from which he required several months to recover.

So when the tragedies stopped, Loren was alone. He wasn't totally well himself, and he had two little girls—one just a baby—to care for. He was very fortunate that his parents were retired and were willing to step in and help him with the girls.

Loren's mother, a godly woman, was concerned about her son's needs. She sent his name to our singles group. He was put on the mailing list, even though he had not yet attended a function. The group sent him all the information that went out to its regular attenders.

Loren didn't attend any of the group's functions for 2 years. "I didn't feel it would be right for me to just take off from my responsibilities as a father and start attending functions as a single. I didn't want to get involved too quickly."

But after a period of time, Loren decided he had better get into a group where he could meet people who could help him. So he began attending FOCAS.

After several months he met a young nurse, Suzanne. In due time they were married, and she became not only his wife but also the mother of his two daughters. Now God has added another blessing to their lives—a son.

The single-by-death person needs the fellowship of other Christians. Yet at this time when his needs may be the greatest of his life, he is suddenly cut off from his close friends. Through no fault of his own, he is now excluded from the fellowship of other married couples. And when he is included he feels ill at ease, as if he were invited only as a gesture. Although he has not changed, his marital status has, and he begins to be left out of a couples' world.

In the Early Church, women who were left

alone were in a desperate condition. Barclay says of that time:

> It was next to impossible for a single or a widowed woman to earn her living honestly. There was practically no trade or profession open to her. The result was inevitable; she was almost driven to prostitution in order to live. (William Barclay, *The Letters to Timothy, Titus, and Philemon* [Philadelphia: Westminster Press, 1975], p. 114.)

We are fortunate today that such conditions do not exist. But because they once did, and because the responsibility of caring for these women fell on the Church, we find specific instructions about their care.

The Early Church daily collected food and goods which were distributed to the poor, the needy, and the widows. The basic physical needs of the widows were provided for.

The needs of widowed persons today may sometimes be physical, and if that's the case it is the duty of the Church to provide for these needs.

But widows also need to feel safe. Crank and obscene phone calls often begin as soon as the death announcement is posted in the newspaper. A woman who may have been sheltered all her life is suddenly thrown into terrifying situations. She needs to feel there is someone to whom she can turn in a time of fear.

The widowed person needs time. This was mentioned earlier concerning Loren. It includes time to adjust to being alone, time to accept the fact that one is single, time for the process of grief to run its course, time to decide to live again, and time to start rebuilding a new life alone.

The widowed person needs the support and fellowship of the Church. Couples don't intend to be cruel and neglectful of the needs of widowed people. It just seems to be a part of the way of life that couples flock together.

But churches do need to reach out to those who are single because of death. Churches need to provide a place to meet their needs.

3

The Needs of Singles

People are the most valuable resource of the kingdom of God and of the local church as well. It is people who help other people. It is people who share the gospel with others, thus ensuring that the good news is propagated from one generation to the next.

The one-third of the people in the United States who are single are too valuable to be ignored, glossed over, or left without any provision to meet their particular needs.

Although the needs of all singles are similar, each age-group has particular needs which must be met. It is up to the leadership of the church to learn the needs of single people and to make adequate provision for those needs.

Let's look at the various needs represented by three age-groups: young singles (23 to 35 years of age), mid-life singles (ages 35-50), and older singles (ages 50 and up).

Young Singles' Needs

Young singles have some needs that are common to married people in this age range (roughly the ages 23 to 35). Some of these are: becoming established in an occupation, learning to handle finances, establishing a home independent of parents, learning to participate in social and civic affairs, and finding a social group that is satisfying.

The young single, more than the older single, suffers great pressure from parents, friends, and acquaintances because of his singleness. The question, "But why aren't you married?" comes up again and again. It may be followed by, "What's wrong with marriage?" or, "What's wrong with *you*?" For the very young single, the assumption is that he is in some kind of transition and will soon find the "right person" and settle down.

Some young people themselves are sure they will marry by the time they are 25. When it doesn't happen at that age, they reprogram for 30, and if that doesn't work, then 35. By doing this, they set themselves up again and again for periods of defeat, self-doubt, and depression.

The 1970 census indicated that 70 percent of the population was under the age of 40. That is a lot of young people, and many of them are single. These young people are mobile, moving from city to city, job to job, and from singles group to singles group. Some of them are searching for life's meaning; some are looking for a mate; some are restless and have untapped energy; some are bored and looking for excitement; some want to get the most possible out of life; some are searching for something new—not sure what it might be.

All of this results in a loose, disconnected kind of life-style for many young singles. It can be very frustrating for those attempting to establish a work among young single people because they may come to the group for a while, then disappear for months, or even years, and you are certain you will never see them again. Then, amazingly, they may return.

Let's look specifically at some of the needs of this age-group.

Becoming established in an occupation. Young single people go through all the problems, joys, frustrations, and sorrows that are common to those attempting to find their first job and become established in it.

For some singles, their job is the center of their lives. They have deferred everything else, even marriage, in order to succeed at it. These highly motivated individuals are usually quite successful in achieving their dreams.

Establishing a home. By the time young people reach 23, most of them have made the decision to have their own apartment or house. At this time, the decision also must be made about whether the individual will live alone or with a roommate.

Loneliness. This is a problem for singles of all ages, but for the young single this may be his first encounter with it.

The young divorced or widowed person may never have been alone at any time before. Solitary living can be a new and frightening experience.

Finding a satisfying social group. For all young people, married or single, it is vitally important to find a social group with which to identify. It is important to begin building the relationships that will later carry them through difficult times of stress. It is vital to have friends who care about what happens to you.

The Christian single needs a place to belong

where he can relate to others who are single and who understand his needs. He needs a sense of family that a Christian singles group can provide.

Finances. Money is a big problem for some young singles who are just becoming established in their occupations. Some have had little previous experience in handling money. They may have the attitude, "Spend it now—who would I save it for?"

Those who are divorced and have young children often have a difficult time financially. Men who have not been given custody of their children have the responsibility of trying to maintain two households. Young single women with small children have to decide whether to work outside the home or to try to make it on limited funds provided by an ex-husband. If they decide to work, they have the problem of finding adequate child care.

Young men, who are more frequently being given custody of at least one of their children, face the same child-care problem.

Participating in civic and social affairs. Young singles are looking for a place to be involved and contribute to bettering humanity.

They are trying to establish their own beliefs, customs, and traditions, and to make their own place in the world, independent of their parents.

The Church can provide a place of service for young singles. It can provide needed training. It must be willing to let the young person make mistakes and then try again.

God's will. The young single is still groping with this area of Christian living. He is seeking direction and purpose. He is looking for God's will in regard to his employment. Some are giving consideration to serving God on a full-time basis. The single may suddenly abandon all he has been so carefully creating and go off to follow a dream or perhaps to answer the call of God.

The young single needs guidance and help in discovering God's will for his life. The Church can lighten his load by providing a place for him to belong, by caring what happens to him, by giving assistance in training, by lending a listening ear, by giving him a meaningful place to serve others, by understanding his needs and frustrations, and by loving him as Christ loves him.

Mid-life Singles

Singles who have reached their mid-life, roughly 35 to 50 years of age, have their own set of needs. It seems that conflicts not resolved in the twenties now become full-scale wars. Tasks that should have been accomplished in the twenties, if left undone, now become gigantic.

By the forties, there are more disappointments; more knowledge that what the single once hoped for may never come to pass. Time just keeps ticking away.

All this can manifest itself in depression, resignation, frustration, and apathy. It is the duty of those who would minister to the mid-life single to know his needs and to provide help in dealing with this vital time of his life.

Those mid-life singles who can get a handle on their lives have the potential for becoming the most productive individuals in the church.

Let's look at some of the needs of this group.

Assuming social responsibility. Learning to

accept his share of social responsibility is an important part of the single's life. The Church can provide an avenue where the single can minister to the needs of others and thereby fulfill part of this need to be socially responsible. Many mid-life singles are looking for a place where they can serve others.

Single parenting. Single parents in this group are facing the same joys and problems of raising teenagers that married couples face, but without the support of the other parent. In fact, single parents sometimes feel their best efforts in nurturing their children are undermined by the other parent. Single parents in the mid-life group need all the help, support, encouragement, and training the Church can give them.

Physiological change. As the mid-life single reaches his forties, he can no longer ignore the changes taking place in his body. Women particularly must now acknowledge the fact that their childbearing years are about over and they may never have any children of their own.

Men, too, must make some changes, although probably not as dramatic as those of women. They need to learn to rely on skill and experience, rather than strength, to accomplish their physical tasks.

Learning how to live with leisure time. Americans have more leisure time now than ever before in history. The shorter work week, flexible time, extended vacations, and job sharing have all contributed to this. It is an area worthy of consideration by leaders of singles programs for the mid-life single.

Psychological needs. The frustrations that

plagued the single in his twenties may now come back with double force. The mid-life single suddenly realizes he or she may never find someone to marry. He may begin to feel life is unfair or that God is unfair. The result will be anger. His anger may manifest itself in a number of ways. He may strike out at others with a nasty disposition, or he may turn his anger inward and become depressed or despondent.

If he has not yet effectively dealt with his loneliness, it will now return bigger than ever. He needs the support of a loving, accepting group of people.

Some have set high standards of achievement for themselves. Now they begin to realize they are probably not going to be able to reach the level of achievement they once hoped for. These are the people in your group who put undue pressure on themselves and others to "do it better."

Unfortunately, divorce takes its toll in this age span. Couples who have stayed together for the sake of their growing children now have no reason to remain together. Some of the singles in your group who have been recently divorced may be full of bitterness, or they may be totally devastated by the experience they have just come through.

Those who have never had a good self-image find this problem intensified in their mid-life years. "What's the matter with me? Why am I still single? Am I ugly? Am I stupid? Why does no one want me?"

The results of a low self-image are never good, and people suffering from it need help.

What are some of the ways we can help the mid-life single?

First, as in all other age-groups, we can provide a place where love and acceptance are the rule and not the exception. This means taking these people just as they are—with all their needs, frustrations, emotional problems, or personality quirks, (maybe even physical disabilities)—and loving them with a self-giving love.

Second, we can give these people help in the area of their need. Counseling should be provided for those with deep-seated psychological needs. Classes and training could be made available to help them handle finances, physical change, and single parenting. They should be helped to improve their skills, whether for ministry, employment, or leisure-time activities. Groups could be formed to study social and civic issues. Other groups could travel and sightsee together.

Third, we can provide a place where they can minister to the needs of others. This can be accomplished through ministry opportunities within the church and also through outreach activities—jails, rest homes, street ministry, or missions. This age-group has the talents, money, and time to make valuable contributions in foreign and domestic short-term missionary ventures. They need to be informed of the opportunities available, challenged to accept them, and organized to do them.

Needs of Older Single Adults

Older single adults, ages 50 and up, also need the support and fellowship of a singles group. This age-group is continually growing, as men's and women's mates die, leaving them single for the first time in their lives. It is a difficult period for these newly bereaved people.

All people at this age begin to meet challenges and changes they have never before encountered. How they meet them depends on the way they have lived up to this point and their attitudes toward life in general. Let's look at some of these changes.

Illness. Many who have experienced good health all their lives now face debilitating and chronic illness. Looking toward years of illness all alone can be frightening to the single person. This is another reason the extended family of a church singles program is important.

Retirement. An overabundance of spare time can be devastating to the person who has spent his whole life wrapped up in his work. On the other hand, to people who are ready for it, retirement can be the most exciting thing that ever happens. It is a chance to start over with a new avocation, such as photography or painting, and make it a second employment pursuit. Retirement can be a time for doing many things the person didn't have time to do when he was working a full schedule.

The happiest retired people are those who are doing something—learning or working—and particularly those who are helping others. Older single people need to have *meaningful* work to do, and the Church can certainly provide that.

Death of a spouse. As we have already mentioned, many become single at this age through the death of a spouse. Generally, women are the ones who are left alone, since men tend to die younger than women.

These women may be learning about their business affairs for the first time in their lives. They may be moving from one living arrangement to another. They may be wrestling with the decision of whether or not they should move in with their children.

Men left alone at this age may have to learn to cook and care for themselves. At a time when the learning process is slower and more difficult, these people have to make major learning changes in their lives. They need the loving support of people who care.

Aging. It is hard for some people to admit they are growing older. These are the people who try hard to keep up with the middle age-group—with little success. They may be ignored, or even insulted, by the younger age-group.

In order to participate with his own age-group, the older single must admit to "being old." That admission comes hard, but it is rewarded by companionship on a slower, more comfortable level.

Social and civic responsibilities. It is estimated that by the year 2000 there will be 65 million senior citizens in the United States. The aged will have increasing political, social, and civic power in this country. If trends continue at the present rate, many of those senior citizens will also be single.

Older people are better educated than ever before. They are more active in politics. Those in politics are staying longer, and other retirees are just entering politics. Single senior citizens need to be informed, active people.

Finances. In an era of rapid inflation, those

living on fixed incomes are the hardest hit. The Church needs to keep a close watch on the general well-being of older retired single people.

It has been the experience, however, of those working with older singles (preretirement age) that they are perhaps the most generous group of all.

Group activities. When planning group activities, the leaders need to keep in mind the importance of planning both an active and inactive program to suit varying physical capabilities.

Most of all, it is important to remember that older single adults are not finished as productive people. The majority have many profitable, exciting years ahead of them—years that can benefit them as people, their singles groups, the Church, and the entire kingdom of Christ.

4

The Opportunities of Singleness—Relationships

Of all the subjects that interest singles, the area of relationships probably ranks first. Single adults want to know how to establish and maintain relationships, how to help them grow and deepen, and how to end them if need be.

Singleness provides a marvelous opportunity to relate to a large number of people. The single has the resources of time and money to invest in friends. He is not locked into a situation where he must relate to only a certain type of people, but is free to get to know a great variety.

Learning how to reach out to others in friendship is a skill. Like so many other skills, it demands time, thought, and practice. It is vitally important that a single learn to relate to others. Friends, to some extent, become his family. He will probably be happy and content with his life in direct proportion to the way he relates to others. A single with a broad base of loving, caring friends will feel content and fulfilled. He will have someone not only to receive from, but also to whom he can give a part of his life.

Biblical Examples

The idea of one person interacting with another

is as old as the story of man. In Genesis 2, God introduced human fellowship with the creation of Eve. He said, "It is not good that the man should be alone" (Genesis 2:18). God never intended for people to live all by themselves. They need to associate with others and live in fellowship and community with one another. In this case He gave Adam a wife, and so began the human race. It would be nice if every person who wanted a husband or wife could have one, but that is simply not the way it is. There are singles who have no desire to marry. Yet all of them need the fellowship and company of other people.

Look at some other Biblical people who related to each other in a deep and lasting way. Can there be any greater love story than that of Ruth and her mother-in-law Naomi? Despite Naomi's repeated pleading with Ruth to remain in the land of her people, Ruth purposed in her heart to go with Naomi. It was a commitment that cost her everything. She left everything to be the constant companion of an aging, grieving mother-in-law. So deep was the relationship between these two women, so great was the commitment, that Ruth could not be persuaded to turn back.

Later her commitment was rewarded by marriage to a rich man and the birth of a baby boy. This child was placed in Naomi's arms as compensation for the sons she had lost. Obed became the joy of her old age. In the Book of Ruth, we read about the attitude of the villagers who said, "There is a son born to Naomi" (Ruth 4:17). Even in this act Ruth took a backseat and let her mother-in-law shine forth. That's friendship!

Consider the friendship of David and Jonathan.

Can we truly comprehend the depth of the relationship which caused these two young men to repeatedly risk their lives for one another? Do we understand a devotion that bears no trace of jealousy? Jonathan, the Bible says, strengthened David's hand in God (1 Samuel 23:16,17).

Jonathan was utterly self-giving in his love for David. There has been, perhaps, no more wrenching parting ever told than that of David and Jonathan recorded in 1 Samuel 20. No greater pathos has ever been penned than David's mournful lament at the death of his beloved friend (2 Samuel 1:25,26).

We are told in the New Testament that one way we know we have passed from death unto life is by the love we have for each other (1 John 3:14). It is the mark of a Christian that he will enjoy the fellowship of other Christians and be willing to commit himself to them, even to the point of laying down his life for them.

Single men need other men to be their friends. They need to be able to share their innermost thoughts and dreams with another man. Single women need women friends for companionship and encouragement. Single men and women both need friends of the opposite sex. They need to know young children and teenagers and older people. They need to know people in the minority races, and the rich and the poor. They need to be able to relate to a wide variety of people.

How Relationships Develop

Relationships begin in a casual way: an introduction, a chance meeting, through a mutual friend or interest, at work. Some relationships develop more quickly than others; some never go beyond the casual stage.

Deep total friendships are rare. These are friendships where one person is totally free to share any dream, hope, or fear with the other without fear of rejection or scorn. These are the kind of friends who do not consider it an imposition to drop anything at any time to come to the aid of the other. In such friendships words may be unnecessary, but each conversation is treasured.

Each new relationship can become a growing experience, as love causes it to expand.

Sometimes relationships between single men and women grow into marriage. That's fun, exciting, and joyful. But it is a pitiful person who enters new relationships with marriage as the only goal. These people miss so much in the process. They limit themselves to one type of experience. They also tend to scare away many persons who could have become good friends.

Factors That Inhibit Relationships

There are factors that can inhibit the establishment of relationships.

People suffering from a physical handicap have a difficult time establishing new relationships. If they are in a wheelchair, the chair itself can act as a kind of barrier to relationships. The blind and the deaf are often misunderstood and may even be falsely labeled as unintelligent. Physically handicapped people can learn to relate to others, but they have to work harder at it. Think of Joni Eareckson and Helen Keller. Both have shown that a physically handicapped person can have good and deep relationships with others.

Some find it difficult to establish a meaningful relationship because they are emotionally handicapped. Broken homes, abuse (both physical and mental), unrealistic expectations, neglect, shyness, and trauma all take their toll emotionally. Some singles have not been able to overcome their backgrounds and suffer from a low self-image.

Another factor inhibiting relationships is that of social ineptitude. Individuals often have had no one after whom to pattern themselves, no model for their lives. They may be crude, boring, or tactless, have bad breath, or wear inappropriate clothing. Their table manners may be deplorable and they may have no idea of the acceptable ways to approach members of the opposite sex.

Such individuals can be taught within the context of a singles group. They can see how others act, dress, behave, think, and speak, and so begin to grow themselves.

Establishing Relationships

How does a single go about establishing meaningful relationships? Procedures may differ, but all are similar.

First, a person who wants to learn how to establish good relationships with others must realize that this is a skill to be developed. He must become aware of his need for this skill. He must decide what behavior on his part will be involved in learning the new skill. He must practice that behavior until it becomes a natural part of his life. He must somehow get feedback on how he is doing.

Susan Dietz, in her column in the *San Mateo Times* (November 7, 1979), listed some rules for relationships. The following have been adapted from her list:

1. Don't cross boundaries that the other person might have.
2. Allow the other person to be himself.
3. Decide which characteristics in the other person you can accept, and those you cannot. To do this, before you enter a close relationship you must be clear regarding your own goals.
4. Try to make it clear to the other person what you are thinking and feeling. To accomplish this, you must understand your own thoughts and feelings.
5. Try not to have irrational expectations of the other person. Do not try to change him in major ways.
6. Take responsibility for your own actions and your own life. Make your decisions for yourself and take the responsibility for doing so.
7. Above all, be kind, courteous, and respectful.

Our rules for establishing relationships could be called the three "Ts" of relationship building.

The first of these is *trust*. Without it a relationship is doomed before it begins. But trust comes slowly. It is built, not discovered. Trust begins with the little things—like an appointment that is faithfully kept, a promise that is honored. Trust should grow to the point where two individuals can share their deepest desires and their innermost thoughts in an atmosphere of acceptance.

Trust is a precious gem. It should never be taken lightly or handled carelessly. Lies, loose lips that share secrets, unfaithfulness in word or action, and an undependable life-style, all serve to break trust. Broken trust may be irreparable.

A person who has suffered a great deal of rejection may find it difficult to take one more risk. But unless the single takes the risk, the relationship will have a difficult time making any progress.

The second "T" is *time*. No relationship can grow unless time is devoted to it. The long conversations that help people know each other take time. Fellowship activities, long walks on the beach, and quiet evenings by a campfire, all require the commitment of time.

"But I don't have that kind of time," some might say. Then we must talk about priorities. If developing new, meaningful relationships is important to you, you must commit time to it.

The third "T" is *transparency*. How many people do you know who live behind a wall of perfection? On the surface everything looks great. There are no problems, heartaches, sorrow, or pain. We are intimidated by such persons. There is no way we can ever hope to attain their level. We have a tough time relating to such people.

But on the other hand, how often do we hide behind the same wall? How often do we pretend nothing ever goes wrong, that we never lose control, that we are somehow superhuman?

Transparency doesn't mean telling all your problems or divulging everything about yourself to everyone. People who tell all, especially in the beginning of a relationship, scare others away. It doesn't mean being argumentative or telling things that hurt other people. Transparency does mean openness, honesty, and self-disclosure.

Joan has dozens of friends. Her formula is pretty simple. "Talk about everything—death, taxes, religion, politics," she says. "So often we avoid these issues. But these are important things and you need to talk about them. Usually by the second time I talk with a person, I'm sharing my personal faith in Christ. Give other people credit for being capable of understanding and caring about what you say."

We soon learn that these people are like us: vulnerable, struggling at times, overcoming, plodding, or overwhelmed by joy. These are real people and they are tremendously appealing.

A relationship founded on trust, time, and transparency should of its own accord begin to deepen and grow. Trust begets more trust. If the time spent together is good, the two individuals will desire more time together.

Deepening the Relationship

Relationships grow as problems and conflicts are solved. Unresolved conflicts have a way of coming up again and again. What may have begun as a very small difference, left unresolved, may grow into a very big conflict.

Confrontation expressed in the proper manner can be very creative. The better two people know each other, and the more they care for one another, the stronger the confrontation will be. The person confronting the other person in the relationship should do so in a judicious manner. He should merely state what he sees as the problem situation and tell how he feels about it and how he is affected by it.

It is well to remember that if you confront others, you must be willing to be confronted yourself. You are not perfect either, and your friends can help you to become a better person.

Sometimes a person will lose when he risks rejection. Sometimes the confrontation may become so heated and the anger so intense that there is actually a split in the relationship. But just because someone is angry with you doesn't necessarily mean the relationship is over. People say things in the heat of anger that they may hardly remember later. You can love someone and still be angry with him.

Repairing Relationships

There are some things you can do to try to repair a broken relationship. One of them is to find out if there truly is something wrong. Sometimes people can go on not speaking to each other and never find out what caused the rift. Perhaps it is all a misunderstanding. Find out by confronting the other person.

Second, apologize when you are wrong. Although this may not totally rebuild the relationship, it is the right place to begin. The Bible says that if our brother has something against us (not us against him) we are to go to him and make it right (Matthew 5:23,24). Some people have a difficult time apologizing to anyone, but an apology is an act of humility that is hard to resist.

Be forgiving if you have been wronged. If someone offers an apology, lay down your anger and accept the apology.

The subject of relationships is vast and complex. We must realize that opportunity for growth lies within our own selves. In the next chapter we'll talk about some opportunities singles have for personal growth.

5

The Opportunities of Singleness—Personal Growth

The single life can be viewed from two perspectives. It can be seen as a sad, lonely existence with little to look forward to but more loneliness. Or it can be seen as an opportunity to use the solitary time to become all God intended the single to be.

Growth will never come to those who sit waiting for something to hit them on the head. Growth comes when we pursue our goals in a logical order to their accomplishment.

Single people can take advantage of hundreds of self-improvement courses. They can attend seminars and conferences on business techniques, dressing for success, and social graces. They can pursue intellectual excellence through adult education. They can study the arts and attend cultural events.

Life With a Purpose

Anyone who has ever accomplished anything had some kind of goal in mind when he started out. Think of Jesus when He purposed to go to Jerusalem the last time (Luke 9:51). Even though He knew the outcome of this journey would be His death on the cross, still He chose to go, so that we could have salvation.

When the heart of the follower is sincere, God has ways of letting that individual know what his goals should be. God also has ways of letting him know when he is off course.

How many people do you know, singles included, who are waiting for a bolt out of the blue to tell them which direction to move? How many purposeless, drifting people have you encountered? Singles easily fall prey to drifting aimlessly through life. Perhaps the lack of responsibility for other people contributes to this, or perhaps they lack input from people who care about the direction their lives are taking. At the bottom of much purposelessness is a lack of self-confidence. "What if I venture out and fail?" "I'm not sure I can do it, so I'll play it safe and not try."

Self-image

There is so much in our culture that wars against a person's self-image. It seems the majority of advertising is geared to make us feel guilty if we are not using some product, wearing some piece of clothing, eating some special food, or driving a certain kind of car. We are constantly pressured to believe the world belongs to the young, the skinny, and the rich. Any one of those three is desirable, but to have them all is the epitome of success.

Well-meaning parents, and some not so well-meaning, have compared one child to another, both within the family and outside it. The intention may have been to spur the youngster to improve, but more often it has served only to devastate the child's concept of himself. Some young people can never do anything right no matter how hard they try. They are constantly harangued, put down, and discouraged.

After a while, they begin to see themselves as dumb, ugly, worthless, lazy, or whatever other definition has been used against them repeatedly. Many singles carry this into their adult lives. Some add social failure and repeated rejection by members of the opposite sex, including marriage partners. Just knowing this is where some singles are coming from will help us to understand their actions and attitudes.

The single can take the first step in overcoming a low self-image by making a visit to Calvary to see what God thinks about his worth.

Gladys Hunt sums it up beautifully:

> Everyone needs to visit Calvary for two reasons: (1) to see the awfulness of our personal sin that necessitated the death of Christ, and (2) to see that God thought we were worth dying for. Both are necessary if we are to understand anything about God's love. Emphasizing either one to the exclusion of the other weakens the value of the one. Understanding both is to comprehend the good news of the gospel. (Gladys Hunt, *Ms Means Myself* [Grand Rapids: Zondervan Publishing House, 1972], p. 16.)

Jesus Christ, who was with the Father when the worlds were created, came willingly to earth to be our Lord and Saviour. He suffered the most humiliating death of His time as a matter of choice, because He felt we were worth it! If that doesn't give us a sense of value, nothing will.

Jesus loves us unconditionally, just as we are. He takes us as He finds us and, through His power, begins to make us what He knows we can be.

If sin is at the bottom of your lack of self-worth, take care of it—be converted. But if it is caused by the mental and emotional garbage that Satan lays on you daily in regard to your value as a person, claim victory today through Jesus Christ and begin to praise Him for His love to you.

Being born again, becoming a Christian, is not the answer to all the complexes that have attached themselves to us through the years. But it is at this point that a person can start to build a new life—free, by God's help, from the weight of worthlessness.

Once the problem of low self-esteem is tackled and is being worked at, what is the next step? Let's go back and talk some more about goals.

Finding God's Will

After a person becomes a Christian, one of his first goals will be to find the will of God for his life. The Christian life is a series of commitments. At each point where a new commitment must be made, there may be a struggle to know the will of God.

The Bible is specific about much of God's will for our lives. There can be little arguing that He wants us to live clean, obedient, upright, honest, surrendered lives. The problems in finding God's will are usually in the area of service. What does He want us to do?

Many Christian people never get down to business with God and find out what He wants them to do. They float through life in a superficial haze. Some are afraid to seek God's will, for they are sure He will ask them to do something they don't want to do.

A wise policy to follow in finding the will of God is to spend a minimum of 5 minutes a day asking God what *He* wants you to do. Too often people talk about wanting to know God's will, they take classes to learn how to discern God's will, and they fret and stew about it, but they don't talk to God about it.

You can know God's plan for your life. God will reveal that plan to you as you walk with Him.

We worry about guidance, but actually that is God's responsibility. Our part is simply to follow without question. Guidance will come when we make ourselves available to God. How it comes is His business. The God who formed the universe can certainly find a way to let us know what He wants us to do.

God has given us brains and He intends that we use them. Some people who set out to know God's will pray about everything—the color of shirt to wear, the kind of food to eat, or which street corner to cross. God isn't as concerned about the color of our shirts as He is about the condition of our hearts.

Even an important decision, such as that made by Paul about where to minister, was first a mental decision (Acts 16:7-10). He made up his mind to go to Bithynia. He used his brain. But he was listening when God told him to go elsewhere.

A good formula to follow is:

1. Examine the principles in the Word of God concerning your situation. Does the Word specifically state the action you should take?

2. Pray about guidance. God, by His Holy Spirit, can give us a deep conviction about the course we should take.

3. Circumstances can guide us. But beware! Some of us know how to manipulate circumstances until we are sure they must be the will of God.

4. Counsel with other Christians about God's will. Again a word of caution: The Bible specifically tells us not to take our counsel from the ungodly (Psalm 1:1). Many people are led astray from God's perfect will by taking their counsel from those who don't know the first thing about the Christian life.

It is wise, too, to counsel with a mature Christian. This is a person who has himself found the will of God, is grounded in the Scriptures, shows wisdom in decisions, and knows how to pray. Such persons will help guide you toward making your own decisions, but will never push you into a decision that could end in disaster.

Above all, remember that the more closely you walk with God, the easier it is to know and do His will. He *will* help you find His perfect will for your life.

Reaching Your Goals

There are undoubtedly many other goals that singles are considering. These may include career advancement, a college degree, marriage, Christian service, financial security, travel, and many others. No matter what kind of goal the single has, it will never be reached until it is broken down into a workable formula.

An example of a workable formula for the Christian is basically this:

1. Make God your first priority and goal. Get to know Him; find out what He wants you to do.

2. Establish measurable goals. What do you want to be doing in 5 years? What goals would you like to achieve by this time next year? What would you like to have accomplished at the end of the next 6 months? 1 month? 1 week? 1 day? You may not reach them all, but you will reach some of them. You will reach more than if you had no goals.

3. Plan a strategy for reaching your goals. Determine what could stop you from achieving your goals. Plan how to set aside that difficulty. Just how will you go about capturing your dream? This is a road map—a plan of action.

4. Set up a timetable. "By this time next month I will have accomplished this much toward my goal, by next year this much, and so on, until I reach my goal."

5. Count the cost. The Bible tells us that no man starts to build a building without counting the cost. Count the cost of your goal in terms of dollars, time, physical strength, emotional energy, mental capabilities. Is this an achievable goal? If it is, or if you think it is, pursue it as if your life depended on it. If it is not an achievable goal, scrap it now.

6. Be aware that there are certain ministry gifts that are supernatural. If God gives you a goal He will enable you, perhaps supernaturally, to achieve that goal.

When a person has established his priorities and goals, his life suddenly lines up. Goal setting and goal pursuit can affect everything about your life-style.

Many singles have reorganized their day in

order to cultivate their goals. Rather than staying up late and dragging themselves out of bed and off to work half asleep in the morning, they realize that a good night's sleep, a wake-up routine with plenty of time, and an alert, cheerful mind will help them accomplish their goals.

Goals determine how money is spent. A woman in a seminar said she was unable to reach a certain goal—travel—because she didn't have the kind of money it takes to travel. Other singles in the group quickly pointed out to her that her first goal, then, was to build up the cash needed to make a specific trip. They suggested working overtime at the job, taking a second job, or developing a more thrifty savings program.

"But what if I set a goal and fail to reach it?" some might say. If you set enough goals you can be assured that at some point you *will* fail. Accomplishing anything in life involves risks or, perhaps restated in Christian terminology, involves faith. Faith is nothing more than stepping out on thin air and letting God put the bridge under you. Remember the Children of Israel who were ordered to cross the Jordan River? They stepped into the water, and when it reached their ankles, *then* it rolled back and presented them dry ground on which to cross. That's risk! That's faith!

Life is an adventure, and most adventures have some risk associated with them. Christians, more than anyone else, should live challenging lives. There is so much God would like to do, and He is looking for people who are willing to venture out in faith and do it.

Living the Christian life demands creativity. It

means being alive and alert to new ideas. It means opening your mind to fresh breezes of imagination. It means dreaming new dreams.

"But I can't!" you say. Yes, you can! As a Christian, you are in contact with the most creative Force in the universe—God. His creative power dwells in you and is available to meet your every need. The secret is in learning how to tap it and put it to work in your life.

Consider the following verses on the subject of God's creativeness: 1 Corinthians 2:12; Ephesians 2:10; 3:20.

Yes, there will be difficulties, problems, and impossible situations. But consider all these as opportunities to see what God can do. Aren't you glad the apostle Paul didn't just give up when he was first imprisoned? During that trying time he wrote letters that help us today. He counseled, encouraged, and took every opportunity to spread the gospel from his prison cell. How many guards, chained to this man as he dictated letters to a secretary, heard the Word and later came to believe on Christ? How many visitors came to encourage Paul and went away encouraged themselves?

If you believe the Bible, you must believe the promise in Philippians 4:19. And if that promise is true, then you can take the risk of living the single life as an adventure, a joy, and a dream to be pursued. You can begin to think of singleness as an opportunity to see what great things God can do for a person who seeks Him and trusts Him completely.

6
The Opportunities of Singleness— Discovering Sexuality

Although we are aware that singles in the world are sexually active, the Church often fails to realize that Christian singles have sexual needs too. Those needs, in addition to traditional backgrounds, the Church's inability to instruct and help, and the pull of the world's attitude about sex and sexuality, all combine to form one massive conflict, which some Christian singles have problems handling.

Some Definitions

Let's begin by defining some terms. First, *sexuality* is all the things that go together to make a person fully female or fully male. Each gender of the human race is vital to the other. Both are God's idea. Both are created in His image (Genesis 1:27).

Masculinity or femininity is more than physiology. It is an attitude—the viewpoint from which life is lived. It is not that one is inferior or superior to the other. It is not that they are equal or unequal. It is that they are different; they have differing gifts. Out of that difference comes the mystery, the excitement of learning about one another.

Coming to terms with your sexuality means being able to admit to being a man or a woman and being glad of it. It is acceptance of yourself as a man or woman and the ability to carry manhood or womanhood with dignity and honor. Fully accepting your own sexuality makes it possible to accept another's sexuality as well.

The term *sex* has come to mean the physical act between a man and a woman. Sex has become a commodity to be bought, stolen, or extorted. Sex, this God-given gift that was designed to be an expression of deepest intimacy between a man and a woman in marriage, has been desecrated beyond imagination by a world totally obsessed with it.

Where It All Began

Sexuality had its start in the Garden of Eden. God created man special, different from the animals. Man was capable of having a relationship, first with God and then with others, and particularly with a woman. Of course, in the beginning there was no woman and God saw that it was not best for Adam to be alone. In another distinct act of creation, He made woman.

God made man and woman to complete one another. They were different, yet so much alike. It was God's idea that they be unique, yet complementary. Where one might be weak, the other would be strong; where one might be retiring and unsure, the other would be confident and decisive. God put within each of them a strong desire for the other. Sexuality is God's design, God's plan, God's idea—and it is good; *very good!*

Singleness had little place in the Old Testament. There were some single people, but the general rule was for Old Testament men to marry and have lots of children. They were to build the human race, and later the Hebrew race. Barrenness was considered a curse from God and caused many a Hebrew woman to cry out to God for mercy.

But in the New Testament we find some notable singles. Of course, chiefest among these was our Lord Jesus Christ. Aren't you glad the Bible tells us He was tempted in all points as we are? He was tempted, yet He did not sin. He was the perfect God-man who understands all about us. He was there when the whole idea was put into operation. He knows us inside and out and is able to do "exceeding abundantly above all that we ask or think" (Ephesians 3:20).

The whole plan began to go wrong when the Early Church fathers started spreading the idea that sex was wrong except for the creation of children. Martin Luther thought the Holy Spirit left the room when a man and his wife had intercourse.

Down through the ages came this attitude that sex of any kind, including that within marriage, is sinful. Then one day the inevitable swing of the pendulum happened, and now we see the opposite extreme which says, "If it feels good, do it!"

Dangerous Trends

It is disturbing to see a trend toward laxity in the area of sexual purity among Christian singles. The problem is that being single does not cancel sexual needs. These needs are still there, particularly for the formerly married who have become accustomed to having these needs met. And the problem is compounded by the tremendous pressures of the world.

But perhaps even more insistent than these, is the longing within the single to be loved; to be held by another human being. One single told us, "I'm going to keep myself pure, but sometimes I just want to scream for someone to please hold me—just hold me."

Some singles will go to any extreme, denying the clamor of their conscience, just to be close to someone for a little while. But these individuals are paying a fearful price for their intimacy. Afterwards some suffer depression and emotional upsets. Some bear children out of wedlock. Some contract venereal disease. All of them experience loneliness when the one-night stand is over—a loneliness and emptiness that cries out for more closeness, intimacy, and sex. It is a never-ending whirlpool sucking them down into despair.

Some who have found no intimacy with members of the opposite sex have turned to a member of the same sex. Homosexuality is a broad topic about which Scripture is very vocal. It is condemned throughout the entire Bible.

What the Bible Has to Say

The entire worldly view of sex today is a far cry from God's original idea. So how does the Christian single who truly wants to live for God put it all together? How does he or she find intimacy without sinning?

The basis for the Christian life is the Word of God. What does the Bible say about the subject of the single and sex? So many times we have to take the basic principles of the Bible and learn from them how to live our Christian lives. The Bible specifically speaks out against fornication. Fornication, the dictionary says, is "sexual intercourse, with mutual consent between two persons not married to each other."

The entire sixth chapter of 1 Corinthians addresses itself to the subject of fornication. (Read especially verses 9 and 18.) God understands and cares about the single person's needs. But most of all, He wants what is best for him, and for the single person the very best is to stay away from fornication and to practice celibacy. Sexual intimacy is for marriage. Anything else goes against God's purposes and is doomed to failure.

People are looking for love, but there can't be love without commitment. One-night stands, or even sex in an ongoing relationship with a special person, does not have the necessary commitment for true happiness. Real love doesn't ask for itself; it gives. It gives what is best for the other person. Real love doesn't take advantage of the situation or the other person's need to be held. Real love sacrifices its own wants to meet those of the other. Real love commits itself totally to the other.

If you take a close look at 1 Corinthians 6, you will see that God has a higher plan for people. Paul says: "Some of you used to do these things, but not anymore. Now you are clean, raised up by Christ's power" (v.11, author's paraphrase). Christ lives within the temple that is our body. He tells us not to pollute this temple by sinful acts. We are to think of ourselves as righteous rulers. We are now in training for eternal service to Jesus Christ the King.

How to Handle It

The way to handle sexual needs is so simple that many people miss it. Follow the directions of the One who created you. If you've made a mess of your life, you can start over with a clean slate. Christ, who is powerful enough to redeem you eternally, is also able to break the habit of sexual sin. He is able to free you from the chains that bind. He is all-powerful!

But even when you are forgiven, the need remains. Admit it to yourself and then to God. There's no use saying it doesn't exist. There's no use pretending you are not troubled by it. Confess to God that you need help. Ask Him to help you.

There is great strength for the person who learns the twofold plan of resisting Satan and submitting to God. The whole idea that "I couldn't help myself," or "the devil made me do it," doesn't hold water. Sure, Satan is powerful. Sure, he tries to make you stumble. But he is nowhere near as powerful as our God, and our God can make bridges out of Satan's stumbling blocks.

Getting to know God, learning to trust Him, and relying on Him totally in the hour of need will stand a person in good stead when the going gets rough. Knowing God and learning to use His strength and power is the answer to every need, sexual or otherwise.

We must realize that we do not have to become an object used to fulfill someone's pleasure. We don't have to buy intimacy. We don't have to pay for self-worth. We don't have to justify our self-doubts by sexual acts. We can be whole, complete, and worthy—because that's what God intends for us.

We must keep our minds from impure thoughts. If we put garbage into our minds, we can expect to get garbage out. Keep putting erotic, lustful material from books, plays, television, or movies into your mind and you will reap a harvest of lustful passions. If we hang around the edges of the whirling cesspool of the world's view of sex, we will eventually be pulled into it.

Be aware that one of the most vulnerable times is after a warm spiritual experience. There is such openness and warmth when sharing God's love that sometimes sexual temptation is heightened. First Corinthians 10:13 is often quoted by singles. Providing a way to escape temptation is a supernatural act of a God who cares.

The answer to handling sexual needs lies not in suppression, which denies their existence, and not in repression, which forces them down into the psyche, but in discipline—self-control.

Discipline is a matter of choices. It says, "I can eat this, but it isn't good for me, so I'll control myself and make a better choice." Self-control says, "I'm angry and I'd like to tell that person off, but I realize it would be a selfish act. It would hurt him, so I'll keep my temper in check." It also says, "I can indulge my sexual desires now, or I can follow God's better plan for me put forth in His Word. I know abstinence won't be easy, but God will strengthen me."

Paul wrote his young friend Timothy to instruct him. He reminded Timothy that God didn't give us the spirit of fear, but of courage and power and love and *sophronismos*—self-discipline. *Soph-*

ronismos is a Greek word defined by Falconer as "control of oneself in the face of panic or passion" (William Barclay, *The Letters to Timothy, Titus, and Philemon* [Philadelphia: Westminster Press, 1975], p. 145).

Reasons People Marry

Sometimes the physical yearnings Christian singles feel cause them to rush headlong toward a marriage for which they are not ready. So intent are they on satisfying their sexual needs that they do not take time to get to know the prospective mate's goals, ideals, interests, preferences, and needs. Marriage is an important step that requires sufficient preparation time.

Why do people marry? They marry for a number of reasons. If you listen to current music, read the testimonials of "famous" people, or view the hundreds of articles and books on the subject of marriage, you might think the only reason for marrying is that people are "in love."

It's interesting to note that "falling in love" is a fairly modern component of marriage. Love was not even considered in the arranged marriages that were customary from the beginning of time until the modern age. Sometimes love happened after the marriage, as in the case of Isaac and Rebekah of the Old Testament, but love was not guaranteed.

It is to the knights and ladies of medieval times that we owe the idea of romantic love. If romantic love is the *only* basis for a marriage and the couple "falls out of love," there isn't much left to keep them together.

Some other reasons people marry are:

To fulfill loneliness. The companionship of marriage is one of its finest assets, but singles who have been alone for a long time might be tempted to look for someone to "make me happy."

On the rebound. People who have been married before are used to being married. Often they miss being married. So they rush headlong into another marital situation before they have fully worked through the grief process that inevitably follows a death or divorce.

They feel sorry for a person. It still happens that some noble persons marry less fortunate people out of pity.

Everyone expects them to marry. They date a few times and people start asking when the wedding date is. Some succumb to this pressure and are swept along straight to the altar.

Pregnancy is still a reason for marriage. About one-fourth of the couples who marry, do so because the woman is pregnant. Feelings of guilt, financial pressures, frustrated ambitions, unfinished schooling, and unrealized employment goals all take their toll, along with an unwanted child.

Some Things to Consider

A lot of what makes a marriage successful happens not in the heart but in the head. And a lot of what happens in the head should happen before an engagement is entered into. Some of the considerations should be:

Do we have common backgrounds? It is a truth that is often discovered too late that you do marry a family when you take a mate. You marry the lifelong training, values, goals, and ideas of that family. If there has been warmth and emotional stability in the home, the end product is usually a warm and emotionally stable person. If there has been stress and upheaval, the person raised in that setting will be affected by it for a lifetime.

Do we have common interests? So often one or the other of a couple thinks, "I can change him/her." But to enter a marriage with the idea that you are going to change the interests or, for that matter, anything else about your partner is a mistake. You will learn to adapt to each other, but usually very little changing will take place.

What about vocational goals? What are you willing to do, to sacrifice, to make those vocational goals a reality?

Can we be friends? Much of marriage is pure friendship rather than passion. If you don't *like* each other as friends, there is little hope for a lasting marriage. Friends share deep feelings, ideals, and goals with each other. Friends are loyal no matter what happens. Friends get under the burden and carry the load for each other.

Do we have common spiritual experiences? Many of the problems people face are basically spiritual problems. Marriage should enhance a person's spiritual life. A relationship with Christ is an extremely personal matter and yet it can be enhanced when shared within the oneness of marriage. This can happen only as both individuals center their lives in Christ.

You should ask yourself some questions about your prospective marriage partner. Does this person have a consistent work record? Does he move about from job to job and place to place, or does he stay put, trying to build something strong? Is he interested in having a family and children? Is this prospective mate capable of warm relationships?

And of course, the most obvious consideration for the Christian single is whether the person is a Christian. This is the bottom line. The Bible is undeniably specific on this subject. Christians are not to be joined with unbelievers in lifelong relationships. To marry a non-Christian is to put yourself in a position of being flagrantly disobedient to God. How can you in the very beginning ask God to bless such a union? He knows the relationship will sap your spiritual strength for the rest of the life of that relationship. For a Christian that means "till death do us part."

God has promised us peace, joy, and happiness through His Son Jesus. But when we step outside His known will and marry an unsaved person, He cannot bless the union.

It is true that many Christian singles have given in to the world's view of sex and marriage. It is too bad because they are the losers. But thank God, it is never too late to change. God, who gave us sex and sexuality, is also able to give us power to live overcoming, wholesome, pleasing lives, and to bless us with fulfillment and joy, regardless of our marital status.

7

Singles in Crisis—Divorce

"What does your church do with people who are divorced?" someone asked. Our answer to that was, "We love them; we just love them."

Those who have not been through the trauma of a divorce can never fully understand the shock, grief, mental anguish, depression, and aching loneliness of a divorced person. We can't understand, but we can try!

There are many women in this country whose husbands will walk into their homes tonight and announce, "I don't love you anymore. I want a divorce." These stunned women will begin to question, to probe for a reason. For some there will be no reason. For others it will be a younger woman, boredom with the marriage, or just a desire for freedom.

There are many men who will return home tonight to find their houses emptied of wife and children. For some, every stick of furniture will have been removed too. Some men will be thrown out of their own homes, and some will arrive to find another man in their bed.

The Phases of Divorce

Divorced people proceed through a series of

phases or steps in their process of recovery. The first phase is *shock*. It is the stunned disbelief that says, "This can't be happening to me. Divorce is something that happens to other people. This must be a bad dream; I'll wake up soon."

People react in different ways during this phase. Some stop communicating and suffer inwardly in silence, wondering what has happened to them. They are torn by rejection, shame, and loss of self-identity. Others go from one individual to another, pouring out their painful story. Some silently cling to the hope: "He will come back"; or, "She'll come to her senses; then we can be a family again."

John told us about his experience: "The aloneness of it was unbearable. I spent as little time as possible at home. The very sight of a family together brought tears to my eyes. Everywhere I turned there was something to remind me I was being denied."

The second phase is the *grieving* phase. Awareness that the marriage is over begins to set in and a grieving process commences. The mourning process is vitally important in the recovery of the divorced person. It can last from 1 to 2 years or longer, but it should not become a permanent part of the individual's life.

Some mourn, remembering all the good things that have happened. This is a positive kind of mourning. Others are filled with self-pity. They are angry and resentful; indeed, some are even violently hateful. This kind of mourning is destructive to the person who engages in it.

Panic is often a part of the early adjustment

time. The divorced person wonders, "Am I going to make it?" Some face loss of income, home, car, or children. They have good reason to feel panic and detachment.

Anger often surfaces during the adjustment period. In fact, most people will at some time experience anger during the recovery period. We have been told that depression and anger are secondary emotions related to some other root cause. That root cause is often one's feelings about himself. One person said, "Satan sits on your shoulder and calls you a lousy, no-good retread."

Lisa felt something different. She felt *relief*. She had suffered years of being mentally and emotionally beaten down until her self-confidence had vanished. But relief didn't spare her from going through a time of depression, grief, and regret for the way things had turned out.

The next phase should be one of *growth*. Over and over, singles who have been through a divorce tell us it became a time of rapid growth in their lives. None of them wanted or would recommend a divorce, but many of them found a way to bring growth out of the wreckage of their lives.

At some time, these emotionally battered people have to realize that what happens to them now will largely be up to them and that they need to take charge of their own lives. Every book we've read and every person we've talked to has emphasized the importance of giving one plenty of time to recover.

Growth will begin when the individual can accept the fact that he or she is divorced—single. He or she must put away the past (particularly when the other person has already remarried) and go on to the future.

The Church and the Divorced Person

It is at this point that the Church can be of tremendous help to the divorced person. One of the ways the previously married person begins to recover and grow is by associating himself with emotionally healthy people who are also growing. If the church has an active ministry to singles, the divorced person has a place to go where he will find others who have been through similar traumas and understand how he feels.

He will also find the spiritual help he needs to begin to grow. Without exceptions, Christian divorced persons relate that it was when they submerged themselves in the Word and called out to God for help that they began to come back to wholeness in their lives.

John told us: "I couldn't sleep nights. But one night I reached a turning point when I began to read Psalm 37 where it says to 'delight thyself also in the LORD; and he shall give thee the desires of thine heart.' Suddenly I realized He wanted to become my source for everything I needed in my life—my happiness, my joy, my companion. That's when I began to live again."

The Bible and Divorce

The Bible says marriage is God's idea and He intends it to be a lifelong monogamous union (Genesis 2:24; Matthew 19:5-8; Ephesians 5:31). That is God's ideal for marriage.

But sin entered the picture, and even in the earliest times divorce happened. It was allowed for a specific purpose: "some uncleanness in her" (Deuteronomy 24:1). But it came to be interpreted that divorces were permissible for almost every cause.

Although it has been allowed, God hates divorce. He hates what it does to people and the confusion it brings into families and relationships. But most of all, He hates the root of divorce, which is a treacherous attitude toward each other.

The Scriptures say God hates divorce (Malachi 2:14-16), but He loves the divorced person. *No one* hates divorce more than the divorced person. Perhaps no one needs to be assured of God's love more than he or she.

Jesus taught about divorce. Read what He says in Matthew 19:8,9. The Church has interpreted this Scripture passage to mean that the only legitimate grounds on which a Christian may seek a divorce are fornication and adultery. Marriage is a lifelong commitment that is not to be entered into lightly and never to be forsaken this side of death.

But what about the person who comes to Christ after a divorce? What about the person who has been divorced but didn't want the divorce? What about the person whose ex-mate has already married someone else? What is the Church to do about these people?

The divorced person who has been asked to withdraw membership because of his divorce sees the Church as cruel and unfeeling, failing him in his greatest hour of need. "Wasn't Christ touched by the *feeling* of the sinner's infirmities?" he asks. "Is there no forgiveness for sin, even divorce?"

"Yes, there is forgiveness for divorce," we say. But sometimes "no" still comes through in the harshness of our attitude.

What about David, "a man after God's own heart"? How could he be called that after he stole his neighbor's wife, committed adultery with her, and had her husband murdered? A man after God's own heart? Yes, after he had asked forgiveness for his sin. Yes, when he was repentant. Yes, after he had paid the price for his sin. He was forgiven and blessed with a special son, Solomon, by that wife. He became the ancestor of Christ Jesus. And David continued to rule with God's favor upon him until his death.

Hard on Divorce, Soft on Love

How should we view the divorced person? A pastor in Texas sums it up well. He says, "We should be hard on divorce and soft on love."

Divorce is not good; it is not what God wants. It should not even be considered by Christians. We should have premarital and marriage counseling, marriage seminars, couples' retreats, and everything else we can think of to strengthen marriage and prevent divorce. But on the other hand, when people come to us battered and bruised by divorce, we should—*we must*—accept them just as they are and love them back to wholeness.

Acceptance becomes easier when we realize that Christ accepted us the way He found us. And some of us were rather unlovely. We too have sinned and no one sin is worse than another; they are all equally bad. Yet He takes us where we are and works with us, loving us to loveliness in Him.

Who are we to think we can do anything less with the singles who come to us, even those who may have caused the divorce? We must start with people where they are, forgive them, and go on from there.

Forgiveness with no strings attached is a wonderful feeling. It takes the load of responsibility for another's actions off your back.

Singles also need love from the Church. They need the kind of love that gives unconditionally. Sometimes they need help with financial problems. Sometimes they need advice from mature Christians on how to raise their children, how to cope with feelings of guilt and loneliness, how to handle sexual feelings, and a host of other problems. But most of all, they need to know you love and care and are available to help them.

Most singles don't want a lot of preachy advice. But knowing there is someone nearby to talk with when the going gets rough is a big help. Sometimes they may just want to talk. Some may need reassurance when their children go off for parental visits with the ex-mate. The people of the church can provide that kind of help. Indeed, how can the Church do less and still show the world we are Christians "by our love"?

Acceptance will breed trust, and trust will help the wayward one grow strong. When he is strong he will try harder than ever not to fail Christ, the individual, or the Church.

It is our observation that the more divorced people you know well, the more compassion you have for them. The more tragic stories of failure and heartbreak you hear, the farther away from divorce you want to stay. The more divorced people that come flooding into your church, the more determined you become to do everything possible to prevent more of this tragedy. The more you watch divorced people struggling to work out their problems, the more you realize divorce may solve some problems but it will raise many new ones in their place.

The influx of divorced people causes pastoral staffs and the lay leadership to become concerned about the status of marriage in our country and to try to do something about it. In our church, the awareness of an increasing number of divorces caused the pastoral staff to implement an extensive premarital counseling service.

What about the influence of divorce on young people and children? Usually young people are accepting and tolerant toward others unless they are prejudiced by their parents to be otherwise. If your children see you caring and being concerned about people in need, they will grow up to be caring, concerned individuals. That doesn't mean, of course, that they will like divorce any better than you do.

Young people in the church need to be taught what the Word of God says about divorce. They need to know why God hates it. They need to talk about the problems that lie in the wake of a divorce. They also need to learn what the Bible says about love. They need opportunities to express their concern to friends whose parents may be going through a divorce.

How totally should we forgive the divorced person? Should we forgive him to the point of allowing membership? Or can we forgive him to the point of allowing him to fill a place of service in our church? Is there a limit to that service?

We have wondered many times in the last few years what we would do without the willing, skilled help of single people. They are a great pool of manpower, ability, and willingness. We are sure we could never get along without them.

However, we do not use divorced singles in the offices of elders, bishops, or deacons. The reason for this is found in the church's interpretation of Titus 1:5-9 and 1 Timothy 3:12. These passages state that the elders, deacons, and bishops must be "the husband of one wife." In order not to err in the sight of God, the church has interpreted these passages to mean that the positions of pastor, elder, and deacon are not to be held by divorced and remarried believers. It is a decision that has been prayerfully made by those in authority as being the truest interpretation of the Scriptures. With the exception of these offices, it is recommended that all other opportunities of Christian service for which these believers may be qualified be made available to them.

Rehabilitation of the Divorced

There is one area we have not yet discussed. That is the question of remarriage of divorced persons. When a singles ministry is instituted in a church, before very long the question of remarriage is raised. It is not an easy one to answer.

The emphasis must be placed on reconciliation whenever possible. If there is even a scrap of hope that the marriage could one day be restored, the divorced person should be encouraged to wait and pray to that end. If the ex-mate has already remarried, and the door is closed to future reconciliation, then the individual should prayerfully seek God's will in the matter of remarriage. Paul encouraged such persons to remain single so they could more fully devote themselves to the work of Christ.

To try to determine who is the guilty one and who is the innocent party in a divorce is not always a simple matter. Only God really knows all the elements involved in the tragedy.

We quote from the bylaws of The General Council of the Assemblies of God, article 8, section 5, which deals with the subject of divorce and remarriage:

> *b. Remarriage.* Low standards on marriage and divorce are very hurtful to individuals, to the family, and to the cause of Christ. Therefore, we discourage divorce by all lawful means and teaching. We positively disapprove of Christians getting divorces for any cause except fornication and adultery (Matthew 19:9). Where these exceptional circumstances exist or when a Christian has been divorced by an unbeliever, we recommend that the question of remarriage be resolved by the believer as he walks in the light of God's Word (1 Corinthians 7:15,17,28).

The position of the pastor and his church should be completely explained to the couple seeking remarriage. If this is done, a misunderstanding and hurt can usually be avoided.

We have met several couples who have been reconciled after a divorce. Al and Doris were such a couple. Al says, "To have a reconciliation you have to let God take control." To which Doris adds, "God has to work on both parties. We know He can!"

After their remarriage, Doris and Al soon had a new ministry. Their hearts were moved by the hurts and problems of singles all around them. They understand those needs and hurts in a way few can. God led them to begin a singles ministry. It is appropriately named "Winners." After 3 years they are still with that group.

If the church is not the place where the divorced individual can seek answers to his questions, understanding for his tears, and compassion for his heart's crying, where can he go? The Church must meet the needs of these people. And they, in turn, must be patient with a Church that is learning, growing, stretching, trying to help them, and trying to meet their needs without falling short of the lofty plans and ideals Christ set for *His bride,* the Church.

8
Singles in Crisis—Widowed

They have been called the "reluctant singles." Widowed people have been catapulted into singlehood by the death of a spouse. Death is certainly no respecter of persons or of age. Death can happen to the young as well as the old. Widowed people are all ages. They need the support, strength, and encouragement of the Church.

As of 1980, there were 10 million widows in the United States. In 1890, the average woman was widowed in her early fifties, but since her life span was short, she died only a few years later. In 1970, a woman could expect to spend 18 years as a widow. Because men on the average die sooner than women, women can expect to live part of their lives as widows. Few of them will remarry, as there are not enough men to go around.

Process of Grief

As you talk with widows, you are struck with the similarity of their grieving experiences. Here we will discuss several areas of the grieving process.

In the initial period widowed persons go into *shock*. This may cause them to act in a calm, collected manner. They may seem to be only slightly affected by the loss of their loved one. There is more shock when the death is due to suicide, a heart attack, murder, or accidental death than there is with a terminal illness.

During the initial shock period the widowed person is carried along by "so much to do." There are decisions to be made about funeral arrangements, relatives to be notified, insurance claims and papers to be filed. Someone must arrange for housing for relatives who will be attending the funeral. Death certificates will be needed for every document and claim related to the death.

Sometime during this period the widow or widower must make some plans for the future. If a man with small children is widowed, he must arrange for the care of those children immediately. Large outstanding debts may mean selling the house, a car, or a business to pay for them.

There are also thank-you notes to write for flowers, food, and service rendered the bereaved. This can turn into a massive job.

At last the funeral is over, the friends and relatives have gone home, and it is time for the widow to get on with life. One of the next emotions a new widow may face is *fear*. Some women have never spent a night alone in their lives. Some fears may have substance. One widow told us that the first night she was alone she received the first obscene phone call of her life. It seems some disturbed individuals read the obituaries and then prey upon unfortunate women.

Soon after the funeral the widowed person must dispose of the deceased's personal effects. Some have no trouble giving away clothing but cling to a toolbox. Most widowed people could use some kind, tender help in disposing of these items. It might make it easier to know some less fortunate person could profit by this gift.

It might surprise those who have never passed through the experience that one of the hardest questions to cope with is the ultimate destiny of the soul of the departed loved one. There may be questions like: "Is there really life after death? Is heaven a reality? Where does the soul go when the body dies? Is what the Bible says about life after death true, or could I possibly have made it up?"

Most widowed people return to their social group thinking they will continue to draw fellowship and support from these lifelong friends. At first the friends are supportive and encouraging, but after a time the widow is not invited to parties where the emphasis is on couples. They don't intend to abandon her, but the truth is that the single person may not fit into the group anymore.

If a woman has been very dependent on her husband, if she has no interests outside the home, if her children are grown and gone, she will have a difficult time adjusting to her single status. Some women have no idea about the financial condition of their families. They have never been allowed to handle money. Suddenly they must face the reality that now they must pay their own way in the world.

Loneliness is a constant battle. Most widows say it is the little things they miss most—water running in the morning as the husband shaves, the intimate chatter in the evening as they compare their day, consultations over small things, shopping together. Women often wish, "I would just like to have someone to hold me and tell me I look nice. No one does anymore."

Guilt rears its ugly head after the death of a loved one. Most guilt is self-inflicted and it must be overcome. Widows suffer guilt when one day they find that a member of the opposite sex looks appealing to them. They feel they are betraying the dead loved one.

Most widowed persons go through a time of *resentment* toward God for taking the loved one. This attitude says, "God, it isn't fair. Why, God, why?" Closely related to this resentment is *self-pity*. "Poor me!" becomes the theme of this person. Unfortunately, some people stay in this period for years.

We like what a young widowed friend, Alese, said about her own grieving process: "I was taught never to feel sorry for myself. That helped me a lot when Bill died. I had also read the Bible all my life and had memorized dozens of Bible verses that helped too. It seemed to me when I read the Bible that there was a time for mourning, a set period, so I decided I would mourn for 30 days and then I would be done with it. I have three small children and cannot spend my life looking back. So that is what I did. I wept and mourned for 30 days, and then I dried my tears and decided to go on with life. I felt that anything more could turn into a sickness that would rob both me and my children of our mental health."

Continued resentment toward God or anyone else has another unpleasant side effect, the growth of *bitterness*. Nothing is more unlovely than a person with a bitter spirit. You cannot be bitter and spiritual at the same time.

Being a widowed person is a new experience, a new stage of life. It can be a time of great personal *growth*. Some men and women would never know the stuff of which they are made if they weren't forced to learn by the death of a spouse. Those passing through this experience should attempt to grow as much as possible.

One widow says, "All of life is a gift from God. Marriage is, motherhood is, and singleness is too." It wasn't until she accepted her widowhood as a gift from God that she began to live again and to grow.

What They Need

The Bible, especially the New Testament, is explicit in its instructions regarding the care of widows. In Old Testament times, women were expected to marry and raise children. When a woman was widowed she usually returned to the house of her father or was supported by adult children. Hers was not a happy lot. Widows of Old Testament times were often impoverished, oppressed, and treated in an unjust manner—but not by God! He became their Champion, Provider, Defender, and Husband.

In New Testament times, things were not much better for the widow. She was still poor. She was still oppressed. But Jesus spoke out against the Pharisees who "devour[ed] widows' houses" (Matthew 23:14).

Jesus was first proclaimed as Christ by a widow, Anna, a prophetess who had devoted her life to God's service. Jesus raised to life the son of the widow of Nain. He didn't seem to make much ado about a woman's marital status. He associated freely with married, unmarried, and widowed women.

In 1 Timothy 5:3-16 strict rules were laid down for the care of the widow. She was, first, to be supported and cared for by her own children and other family members. If there were no family members to care for her, it was the duty of the Church to care for her. There seems to have been a society for widows who were ready to devote themselves totally to the service of the Church. These women were to be at least 60 years old, have been married only once, and be known for their good works. Paul preferred that the younger widows remarry and continue their domestic lives.

One of the greatest needs of widows today is *a place to serve* within the church. They need to be *encouraged to develop an attitude that honors Christ*. The testimony of one who has been bereaved and has grown in Christian grace because of it is powerful. She needs to be encouraged to reach out to others.

Widows sometimes want to stay within the walls of their homes where they find solace and safety. They do need to be *encouraged to get back into the mainstream of life*. So many widows we have talked to say reentry happened when they began to reach out to others.

They need to be *encouraged to pursue a new lifestyle*. A widow may need more schooling. Now there are many reentry programs for both college and job training. She may need to update her job skills and be encouraged to reenter the job market.

The widowed need time to grieve. Some well-meaning individuals have thought they were helping when they encouraged the widowed person to remove his/her wedding band and "get out and see someone." The widowed need your concern but not your pushing.

The widowed need your faith in their ability to cope. They need you to believe in their strength. One widow had been a very dependent wife. Her life had been tailored to her husband's in every way. When she lost him, she was devastated. She began getting notes in the mail from a friend, saying, "You can do it. Hang in there." These notes, which came often during the first 6 months, were just what she needed to encourage her to take up her own life.

Recovery

The recovery period for a widowed person starts about 3 months after the death of the mate and can last from 1 to 5 years, with the average being about 2 years. It is a time of learning to let go of the past and starting to rebuild a new life.

Over and over again Christian widows emphasize the importance of the Bible in their lives. Some have found new life and strength in the psalms. Suddenly the words, "Though I walk through the valley of the shadow of death, I will fear no evil" (Psalm 23:4), take on new meaning. The loved one has walked through death's door, and it has slammed shut with finality.

After a while the widowed person begins to feel he is recovering. Now there are some good days, and the time between bad days is growing longer. Then, without warning, something will remind him of the lost spouse and a floodgate of tears is opened. A young widow said, "Sometimes I cry into my pillow. I'm so lonely I feel like I'll die."

William E. Denham, Jr., in an article titled "Coping With Grief," lists some valuable guidelines for the bereaved. (*Christian Singles* [Nashville: The Sunday School Board of the Southern Baptist Convention, July 1979]:17-19.) The following guidelines have been adapted from his article:

1. Accept grief as *given* in your life.
2. Stay in touch with your emotions—do not deny or ignore them.
3. Do not make any new romantic attachment quickly. Emotions need time to heal.
4. Be aware of your anger. Recognize it and choose an appropriate way and time to express it.
5. Allow room for guilt.
6. Face your grief. Allow yourself to measure all of its dimensions.
7. Allow your grief some time.
8. Utilize your network of support. Explore relationships you may not have needed before.
9. Don't ignore deep depression. Get help—see a counselor or physician.
10. Believe in the future—*hope*.

How Can the Church Help?

The Church can help widowed persons in a number of ways. It can help by encouraging them to trust in God. The widow must be encouraged to move on from her place of sorrow into the wider life that God has planned for her. She must have a basic trust in God to help her take the first step. Widowhood is an opportunity to grow and to find fulfillment in a new and exciting life.

The widowed person needs to be encouraged to be thankful in everything. That means being thankful that God in His all-loving wisdom thought it best to take the beloved spouse. But some have trouble being thankful that they are left behind to cope with a life that has now lost its appeal.

What the church should do is equip women to become widows, but such classes would probably not be very popular. The next best thing is to teach widowed people how to cope. Such courses might include: how to balance a checkbook; how to repair a light socket, a faucet, a washer, etc.; how to service a car; how to drive; and so on. There could be sharing and support groups to help the widowed cope with emotional problems.

The church can help the widowed person by avoiding classes or events that are "for couples only." This would help not only the widowed, but also divorced and never-married singles who might enjoy fellowshipping with friends in these groups.

Individuals in the church can help by becoming aware of a widowed person who is sitting alone in a pew. If someone would sit with that person, it would help greatly. It is not easy to sit alone after years of having a loved one alongside.

The widowed person finds it easier to stay home than to go alone to a church event. He fears he will find himself standing alone in the middle of a large room with no one to talk to. A couple could make it a point to take a widowed person to a church social event, stay nearby all evening to make sure he is not awkwardly alone, and then take him home at the end.

Keep the channels of communication open between the widowed person and the singles program of the church. The newly widowed person probably will not want to participate in a singles group for a while, but he may sometime in the future. It may take 1 or 2 years before he feels a need for the group.

Encourage the lay leadership of the church to care for the widowed. The church should be sure its widows are provided for in a financial way if that is necessary. The lay leadership should care for this group of people.

The widowed person may need guidance about living quarters and disposal of personal property and goods. He needs time to make a major decision about where to live and what things he will still need. Eventually changes should be made. Life goes on. It can be healthy to redecorate the house and dispose of items that are no longer useful and serve only to depress the widowed.

The widowed should be encouraged to set new goals. A friend and her husband were planning to return to the mission field when he died suddenly of a heart attack. After about 15 months of going through the grief process, she was ready to try her solo wings. Her foreign missions board reassigned her to the Far East, where she is serving today.

God may have a new set of marching orders for the widowed person. He does all things well, and in taking a loved one He has a better idea for the person left behind. If the widowed person can be encouraged to look to God for His perfect plan, in time it will be revealed. A whole new life—an exciting, fulfilling life—may be just ahead.

9

Singles in Crisis— The Single Parent

The telephone at Alese's house rang one evening 4 years ago. Bill, her husband, had been killed in an automobile accident. In a moment's time she became a single parent with three dependent children, ages 5 months, 18 months, and 5 years.

Jim became a Christian a number of years ago. But his wife never made a commitment to Christ. Eventually she filed for a divorce. When the county official came to interview Jim, his wife, and their children, he shook his head and said, "I don't know what to do about custody of the children. You're both good parents." Jim refused to draw his children into a court battle, so he relinquished custody. About a year later his wife awarded custody of their son to him. Now Jim is a single father with custody of one of his two children.

Donna was sitting in a living room chair, her leg propped up after surgery. Nearby one of her three children, a nursing baby, was sleeping in a crib. Donna's husband walked through the door and announced his intentions to divorce her.

These are only three of the 8 million one-parent households in the United States in 1980. These eight children are numbered among the estimated 13 million children under 18 years of age in one-parent households. Ninety percent of those households are run by women alone. However, this figure may change as more fathers are given custody of their children. Approximately 1 million children each year are involved in the divorces of their parents.

Who Are They?

Who are the single parents? They are people who come from all walks of life. They live in every neighborhood, and they all thought it could never happen to them—but it did. The divorced and the widowed are stunned into reality one day when they realize they are left alone with children to raise. There are single parents who are separated from their mates because of marital difficulties, military or business reasons, or because one parent is institutionalized.

Divorced Parents

Divorce is a traumatic time for parents and children alike. Even as the parent does, so the child too feels shock, depression, denial, anger, low self-esteem, and anxiety. Often little children between 6 and 8 years of age feel they somehow caused the divorce. Older teens tend to have a pervasive sense of sadness and have many problems with loyalty to one or both parents.

The newly divorced parent must deal not only with his own shock and despair, but also with that of his bewildered child. At a time when the parent may be almost nonfunctional because of depression, the child is crying out for answers, security, and self-identity. Both the parent and the child think they caused the divorce and are carrying their individual load of guilt. At a time when the parent would like to run and hide, to lick his wounds, the child, who has lost one parent, fears that he will lose the other one as well. Often it is too expensive to maintain a large home. That means resettling the family in smaller quarters—another stressful change for the child.

Someone summed up the frustration of single parents by saying, "The problem is too much child, and too little time and money to raise that child." That is true for the custodial parent. Meanwhile, the other parent aches with loneliness for companionship with the child. To make up for lost time, he or she may come bearing gifts. This is further resented by the custodial parent, who often cannot indulge the child and can think of so many practical places the money could go.

Widowed parents suffer many of the same problems as divorced parents. They too go through a time of shocked disbelief. They deal with worry and fear in their children. "Mommy died. What will happen to me if you die too?" the child might ask. The parent is grieving over the loss of a mate and is having to cope with the child's grief as well.

But there are notable differences. The Church tends to rise to comfort the bereaved. There are warm expressions of sympathy and pleas to "let me help you." The widowed person is not made to feel second class or rejected.

Both divorced and widowed parents express similar concerns for their children. Mothers ask, "How do I teach my son to be a man? How will my children learn about loving relationships between a man and a woman? How will they know how a family works together and relates to each other?"

Separated Couples

There are couples whose marriages are troubled and they have decided to separate but not to divorce. Sometimes these trial separations end in divorce; sometimes they become more or less permanent. Single parents in these circumstances face much the same problems as divorced people.

But there are other kinds of separation. One parent may be permanently hospitalized or institutionalized in a prison or a mental institution. Then there are those people who are separated by occupation, military service, or other business involvements. These are single-parent families at least part of the time. Their needs should also be considered.

Concerns and Problems of Single Parents

Most single parents are simply overloaded with responsibility. They have little strength to spend helping their children with homework, playing games, or even teaching them how to work.

The children may be angry with God. "I prayed and prayed, but Mom and Dad got a divorce anyway. Doesn't God care about me?" It may take patient, loving understanding to bring the child out of his anger. Older children, having suffered a loss of identity, may go looking elsewhere for a new one. They may take up with a new peer group, do things they have never done before, or rebel against all authority.

A never-ending problem for the divorced parent is dealing with the ex-spouse. When children are involved, one divorced parent is never through dealing with the other one. Every time a child makes a noncustodial visit the hurt can be reactivated. It is particularly hard for a noncustodial Christian parent to see his child being raised in a non-Christian environment.

Some single parents are trying to be both mother and father to their children. It just can't be done. The only result of this action will be a lot of guilt and frustration.

Relationships with grandparents can be difficult and strained for the ex-spouse. But the children have a right to know their grandparents and can benefit from a continued relationship with them. It will give their life a sense of stability.

Then there is the whole area of "blended" or "reconstituted" families. The problems of stepparenting are complex and contribute to the poor success rate for second and third marriages.

What Does the Bible Say?

The Bible is full of admonitions for the care and feeding of widows and the fatherless. God cares for those who are left alone to raise children.

Elisha encountered the widow of a student prophet. (Read the story in 2 Kings 4:1-7.) God provided for a single parent and her children.

Proverbs 15:25 says the Lord will "establish the border of the widow." *He* sets up her house. *He* helps her raise her children. *He* gives her strength to cope. (Also read Jeremiah 49:11.) God is the defender of the single parent!

God is able to cause the single parent to stand in the face of crushing problems (Psalm 146:9). The single parent can take hope from this psalm for here is a Helper, God, who keeps His promises.

Jesus had some encounters with single parents. Remember when He stopped a funeral procession, raised a dead son, and gave him back to his widowed mother? Remember Jesus' concern for His own mother while He was on the cross? In one of His last statements, He gave her into the care of His beloved friend John.

From the Scriptures we can conclude:

1. That you need not fail.

2. That you are not alone—Jesus is the protector of single parents.

3. That you can't sit around waiting for the church to take care of you. No one owes you anything. Often the church doesn't know the needs because single people let pride keep them from sharing their hurts and needs with others.

4. That the Lord does not want you to suffer from guilt. Yes, you may be partly at fault for a divorce, but Christ can erase your past.

5. That feeling sorry for yourself accomplishes nothing.

6. That blaming yourself, your ex-spouse, or others is not good. Rather, you are to "trust in the *Lord* with all your heart."

A woebegone, "poor me" attitude is the most useless, debilitating attitude a single parent can have. Read Hebrews 12:12,13. Did you notice who is to straighten the path? *You are!* You do it!

God has a plan and a purpose for the single person's life. The single is to serve God in the midst of his troubles and God will not fail him.

Fill your mind with positive thoughts and teach your children to do the same. Set new personal and family goals. With God's help, you can.

Helping the Children

There are some things you can do to help children who have been through a divorce or death:

1. Give the child time to heal. You need that time; he does too.

2. Be honest. Tell the child exactly how you feel without being hateful about the other parent.

3. Accept the child where he is. If he's struggling, accept him in the same way you would like to be accepted.

4. Give him comfort. Don't be so concerned with your own needs that you forget the child needs comfort too.

5. Give the child encouragement. Encourage him to continue pursuing his goals.

6. Be strong in your faith. This is not the time to abandon the church.

7. Be patient. The child may be angry, frustrated, grieving, and miserable to live with. But what is happening isn't his fault and you need to be patient with him.

8. Let the child share responsibility in the home. You'll need his help now more than ever. But beware letting him become a substitute spouse.

9. Have fun together. Do things together, play together, and laugh and talk together. Fun can be a great lightener of heavy loads.

10. Let the child know he is loved.

11. Let the child know there will always be someone to care for him. He won't be left alone.

Donna says, "Singles have an advantage. You must be an example to your children. You don't teach children what you don't do yourself. You are forced to grow."

The Church and the Single Parent

There are a number of ways the Church can minister to the needs of single parents. First, we must not judge them. They need someone to reach out to them in understanding, to believe in them.

One single parent told us that if the pastor just mentions the words *single parents* in a sermon this encourages him.

Another single parent said, "We're singles, but our needs differ from those of the other singles. Because we have children, we cannot participate in as many activities as singles do. We have to think first of the well-being of our children."

The single parents of one church have solved the problem of being different from other singles and other parents by forming a single parents club. Their meetings are designed to bring encouragement and information on parenting. Special speakers are often invited to give some expert guidance. It is a spiritual base from which children are being influenced for Christ.

We can also include single parents in our circle of friendship. In this way, their children can learn in a natural, unforced way how other people, and Christians in particular, relate to one another.

Christians can realize that single parents need to get away from their children at times. They need to take care of their own personal growth through seminars, retreats, and just plain relaxation. An offer to keep the children and free the single parent is a valuable Christian service and a gift that will be appreciated beyond measure.

Single parents should take advantage of already-established programs for children. Educational programs such as Sunday school, vacation Bible school, camping, scouting, and other similar programs are a natural place for one-parent children to relate to other children and to Christian men and women.

We must realize that if one child or one parent is helped, all the efforts the church has put forth are worthwhile. You cannot help all the one-parent children of the world, but you can see that one child gets your attention.

The church can spend some money for books on single parenting for the church library. Men can be encouraged to take an active role in the church's programs for children. Their influence on these young children cannot be measured.

Sunday school teachers and workers with children should be made aware of the grief process through which a child passes when a divorce occurs. Just knowing this, will help these workers understand when a child is moody or misbehaves to get attention. Even though he understands that the child is going through a period of adjustment, the misbehavior cannot be overlooked. Some children adapt to their new circumstances rapidly with seemingly little or no problem. These children are called the "survivors" by family professionals. They have a strong survival instinct and push aside negative circumstances.

The church that cares for the fatherless, widows, and single-parent families will be rewarded by the God who watches over them.

10
The Church and Singles—Establishing a Singles Ministry

With the singles population increasing daily, the need for ministry to them also increases daily. While you are deciding whether or not to begin, thousands of singles are being added to the total.

In 1968, a handful of single adults came to Frank Schneider, Director of FOCAS ministries at Calvary Temple in Seattle, Washington, and asked him if he would consider beginning a class for them. Frank felt the need and accepted the opportunity. It was not a large beginning—only six people—but it was a start.

After a slow and sometimes discouraging beginning, the decision was made to move the group to a neutral setting, a restaurant. As soon as that move was made, the group began to grow.

From that humble beginning has grown a continuing ministry to thousands of singles in Seattle and the Pacific Northwest region. Multiple groups now exist to meet the full scale of needs represented by the single-adult attenders. The annual singles conference is attended by as many as 1700 singles.

Identify Your Singles Population

Probably there are already a number of singles

in your congregation. To identify singles, register every attender with a census card. Somewhere on the card, along with the name, address, telephone number, and zip code, there should be a place for recording whether the person is single or married.

Secure an Advisor-Overseer

This person is the key to a successful beginning of your single-adult program. He or she should be someone who is willing to make a total commitment to the singles group. The advisor-overseer provides stability and continuity to the group. Single adults tend to be highly mobile. Therefore, the advisor-overseer must be deeply committed to the group and faithful in attendance and in representing the group. He must be a consistent, spiritually mature individual.

It is also the function of the advisor-overseer to keep the standards of the sponsoring church before the singles group. A singles group that is functioning well draws people of all faiths and backgrounds. This makes the ministry very evangelistic. It also introduces many standards, cultural backgrounds, and religious traditions into the group. This could result in conflict within the group or between the group and the sponsoring church. The advisor-overseer lays down the policy and explains the position of the sponsoring church. The advisor acts as liaison to other pastors, the church board, and the church body. He speaks for the group and represents their interests in church business meetings.

The advisor *does not* run the singles program. Single people are adults and are fully capable of designing and operating their own programs. Doing everything *for* them is demeaning and makes them feel like second-class people.

Single people have a great deal of free time. They need lots of activities to fill that time. It would be impossible for an advisor to attend every function held by the group. It should be understood from the beginning that the advisor will not be at all functions. He should randomly attend outings the group may conduct, but in no way should he try to do it all.

The advisor, however, does need to be accessible when it comes to acting as a counselor, friend, and prayer partner. He must be a compassionate person who is ready to listen whenever the need arises. The advisor needs to be a person of faith and prayer. He needs to know his limitations in the area of counseling. There will be problems too complex for him to handle and he needs to turn the counselee over to a trained Christian counselor for long-term counseling.

Choose Facilities

There are several possibilities for meeting places for a singles group. First, they can meet within the church. This has advantages in that people usually know where the church is and it is convenient to attend. Second, for parents with small children, it is a simple matter for them to drop off their children at their own Sunday school classrooms in the same building.

The second choice of facilities would be a neutral setting, such as a restaurant near the church. The advantages are that people who might not come to a church would feel free to attend a class held in a restaurant. Divorced single adults who have been hurt by the church's attitude toward them might feel freer to participate in a neutral setting. Experience has shown that singles groups grow faster in a neutral setting. Singles from all types of churches will gather for fellowship and learning and then return to their own churches to worship.

Set up a Simple Organization

Keep the organization simple. You can start with a teacher-advisor and a handful of people for a Sunday school class. But even at this earliest stage, the class should have its own officers. It is important that as many people as possible be involved.

The first two officers chosen should be a chairman and a cochairman. The first chairman serves his term; then the cochairman assumes leadership. At this time a new cochairman is chosen. The cochairman is, for all practical purposes, in training to become chairman of the group. This system makes for smooth transition of leadership.

The advisor, chairman, and cochairman form an executive committee. Their function is to discuss goals, ministry appointments, and how to implement the decisions of the planning committee. Other officers may be added as the group grows in size or as individuals feel the need for expanded ministries. Given below is a listing of possible ministry positions you may wish to add to your group:

Recording secretary—keeps minutes and performs secretarial duties.

Corresponding secretary—sends welcome letters to all new visitors. Writes thank-you notes and other necessary correspondence.

Treasurer—collects, records, deposits, and reports all financial activities of the group.

Fellowship or social chairman—offers planned activities of a spiritual and recreational nature.

Spiritual-life chairman—coordinates prayer and Bible-study groups.

Caring chairman—assists singles within the class during a time of need with Christian love and concern.

Outreach chairman—institutes, coordinates, and facilitates projects that reach outside the group itself—such as nursing homes, hospitals, jails, missions, etc.

Publicity chairman—gets the word out to the public through newspapers, radio, etc.

Membership chairman—maintains files on all participants. Plans follow-up methods.

Music chairman—promotes spiritual climate through music in the class and at social functions.

Calendar chairman—gathers calendar information and organizes, prints, and distributes it.

Hospitality chairman—oversees welcoming visitors, makes sure room is ready, calls first-time visitors, and coordinates phoning for special events.

Arrange for Finances

You will be amazed at how quickly a singles program is able to pay its own way financially. However, in the beginning the group will need some assistance. The church should consider this expense as an investment in souls.

The singles group should be encouraged to become self-supporting as soon as possible. This can be done through the use of offering envelopes printed specifically for the group. The reason for this is that it is healthy for a singles group to have their own finances. This instills in them a sense of responsibility for their own group. Arrangements can be made for petty cash funds to be available for each group, but they should deposit all funds and write checks whenever possible as a record. The group should be encouraged to share in missionary projects and other giving projects.

Plan the First Activity

Choose something that will instantly involve everyone who comes. A potluck dinner or a picnic will involve everyone because each person must bring some food item. Whatever you choose, make it a warm, informal, pleasant occasion. At this meeting, set the date for a regular meeting time.

Next, begin to work with the singles in planning publicity. Ask them how they think the new ministry should be publicized. Use the church bulletin, the local newspaper, and business cards, but emphasize to all that the best advertising is word of mouth.

Choose a *good* Bible teacher for the first series of meetings. Emphasize to the teacher the importance of solid Bible teaching, firmly based not on problems and solutions, but on the Word of God. As the individual is built up in faith through hearing the Word, he is able to solve his own problems. This is a positive, uplifting kind of teaching that will help members of the group become steadfast in their faith.

Pray about your group. Pray with the singles about leadership for the group. It can make all the difference in the world. This first nucleus becomes your new leadership. They must make decisions regarding the group. They must reach out and tell other singles that they exist.

Plan Succeeding Activities

After the initial meeting, gather the core group together for a "planning council." This council is open to anyone attending the group who wishes to participate. This gives a feeling of openness and conveys a desire to include as many people as possible.

The advisor plays an important part in the planning meeting. He makes sure that all plans align themselves with the standards of the sponsoring church. In order to plan to meet single-adult needs, the advisor must first know those needs. The advisor should make a thorough study of the needs of single people. He should not assume that he already knows them.

It is important to include something for everyone. Older or physically impaired people may not be able to participate in some activities. Always make allowance for them. Remember to include the children of single parents in some events. There are more and more single parents. They should be able to have their children with them part of the time.

The activities chosen by the group should not be so costly that they exclude single people who are living on fixed incomes or limited budgets.

A variety of activities will provide something

for everyone. The wider the variety of activities, the more individuals to whom you will appeal.

The Sunday school hour is probably the most important part of your singles program. It deserves some careful attention to detail. It is essential that you prepare all details ahead of time. There should be a guest register and someone to handle it. It is vitally important that the name, address, zip code, and telephone number of every attender be recorded.

It is helpful if every person has a name tag. First-time visitors should be considered "first-timers" or "new friends." You should never allow anyone to refer to them as "visitors."

Other support people might include someone to take attendance. Also, a host and hostess should get there early to welcome people as they arrive.

The Sunday morning hour should include: fellowship, singing, worship, announcements, and the lesson. Other activities may include testimonies, special music, and occasionally, a whole morning given to a prayer-and-share time.

Many other activities can be carried out on weeknights, Saturdays, or Sunday afternoons:

Potluck dinners
Boat cruises
Hikes & biking
Volleyball games
Gym nights
Singspirations
Drama
Concerts as a group
Crafts
Car rallies
Picnics
Table-game nights—good for winter
Slide and movie presentations by members
Active sports—skiing, sailing, bowling, etc.
Talent nights—musical groups can perform
Celebrating special events—Christmas, Easter, birthdays, etc.

In addition to these events, the group can hold one or two retreats each year. These should be well planned. Secure the finest speaker available and plan to pay him well. It can mean the difference between success and failure.

Another idea might be to have small modules or learning groups. These are formed for a short period of time and provide an opportunity for learning and fellowship. Some modules could focus on: bachelor cooking, car mechanics for women, Bible study, photography, and "special-interest" groups.

Specialized topics, those of interest to only a small segment of the group, can be dealt with in seminars. Some suggested subjects might be: divorce recovery, single parenting, learning to live again (for widowed persons), and time management.

The Monthly Calendar

Every event planned by the singles group must be put on a monthly calendar. Each person *must* receive a copy of this calendar. Therefore, the mailing list should be extensive and should be growing week by week. This is why a guest register, signed with each person's full name and address, is so important. This mailing list becomes the group's lifeline.

Remember that singles in a warm, loving, caring group draw other singles. If they find love and acceptance, they will stay and become a steadfast part of the group and, in turn, reach out to more single people.

11
The Church and Singles— Expanding the Singles Ministry

"Even if you don't need the group, the group needs you!" someone said at a singles leadership-training retreat. That statement is full of implications for expanding your singles ministry.

It is important to recognize that many singles come to a singles group because they have profound needs: they are hurt and need healing; they are lonely and are looking for fellowship. If your group is a caring, ministering body, these needs will be met. But often when the single's needs are met, he loses his incentive for attending the group. New incentives need to be offered. One of the best is to feel needed and to have ministry to the group.

Leaders need to understand the stages through which singles pass in relationship to the group:

1. *Searching*—there are singles in your area who are desperately in need of your group, but don't know it exists.

2. *Pondering*—there are singles who have heard about your group and are contemplating attending.

3. *Nibbling*—in this stage the single decides to attend some function of the group to see if it can meet his needs.

4. *Participating*—the single decides the group can help him and decides to participate on a fairly regular basis.

5. *Growing*—the single has his needs met and the original reasons for his attendance are no longer there. If we don't provide a new purpose, this person is likely to drop out or become sporadic in his attendance.

How do we do this? We have attempted to think of the group in terms of concentric circles of involvement.

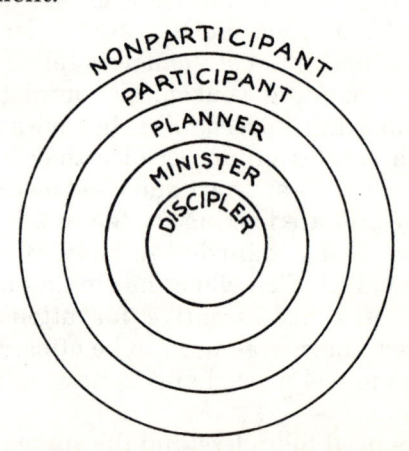

(Concentric circles, from outer to inner: NONPARTICIPANT, PARTICIPANT, PLANNER, MINISTER, DISCIPLER)

Circles of Involvement

The *nonparticipant* has made no commitment to the group. However, he has allowed his name to remain on the mailing list and he continues to receive information about the group.

The *participant* has made a commitment to attend functions of the group and is receiving ministry from the group. He is basically concerned about *his* needs being met and, as long as they are, he will continue to attend. We must be careful that we don't put the participant in a dependent relationship that keeps him attending but does not help him to grow.

When a participant commits himself to help as a *planner* he has entered a new dimension of involvement. From being ministered to, he moves to accepting responsibility for ministering to others. This is an important step. With this commitment comes a surge of spiritual growth and maturity.

When a person on the planning council accepts an assignment, whether it be to greet new people who come to class or to type the class bulletin, he moves from planner to *minister*. Once a person has accepted an assignment, he is usually never again content to be just a planner or participant.

The inner circle is for *disciplers*. To reach this level a person must visualize himself not only as a minister, but also as an encourager helping others to find a meaningful place of ministry.

It is important to always have something more ahead of growing people. Some singles who have leadership drives need to be given opportunities to fulfill these desires. Some singles need to be given opportunities to develop new areas of ministry beyond the group.

Involving Singles in Ministry

The first level of involvement is *participating* in the class group. The only commitment is a decision to attend class functions. The second level of involvement is *planning*. We encourage all the class attenders and newcomers to participate in the planning council. It helps them understand the purpose and goals of the group.

Hopefully this contact will inspire them to the next level of involvement, *ministering.*

We want as many singles as possible to take on a ministry. It is important that the leader share with the planning team the spiritual criteria for being a worker for God. We do not advocate giving leadership ministries to those who are not born again. We have, however, allowed non-Christians to participate in some forms of ministry while working in tandem with born-again Christians. Some of these ministries might be to help with mailings, organize parts of a social activity, or help with hospitality duties. The non-Christian is often drawn into the kingdom of God as a result of his participation.

Here are some important things to remember regarding ministry by singles to singles:

1. *We need to realize that ministry is the function of all the people of God.* (Read Ephesians 4:16.) We must allow everyone to experience the thrill of serving God in the ministry to which God has called him. The more singles that are involved in ministry, the more your group will grow—both in numbers and in spiritual maturity.

2. *We need to realize that God wants every Christian single to be a minister.* (Read Ephesians 2:10.) God wishes each person to fulfill certain ministries for Him. Leaders need to help each single discover what his talents are and find a place in the group where they can be expressed.

3. *We need to realize that singles have a God-given desire to minister.* (Read Philippians 2:13.) How leaders visualize singles in the group is important. If we visualize them as being internally motivated by God and needing only opportuni-

ty and direction to get started, we will have an exciting group on our hands.

4. *We need to realize that many Christians have a natural hesitancy to minister.* Call it the "Moses mentality," which says, "Lord, I can't speak. Send someone else who can do it better than I can!" or the "Gideon complex": "Lord, who am I? ... I'm not qualified." Jesus said that a certain amount of hesitation is good; He called it "counting the cost." But He spoke against other kinds of hesitation which were not well-founded, such as, "I must first bury my father."

Our role as leaders is to help singles see what is involved in a ministry. We must help them count the cost—how much time is required, what skills are needed, and how much energy, strength, and money it will cost. Then if we feel they should pursue that ministry, we must encourage them to respond. We need to stir up each person's God-given desire to minister and provide him with a climate of support (Hebrews 10:24).

If leaders want their singles ministry to grow, they must allow each single person to minister within the group. Leaders will not lose their jobs by doing this. In fact, members of the group will be drawn closer to the leaders when they experience the joys of ministering. They will be able to sense the throb and flow of the Spirit as He anoints them in the work of God, just as He has anointed the leaders. They will learn to ask God for solutions to problems and frustrations. They will feel the thrill of joy when prayers are answered and the work goes forward again.

How can leaders challenge singles to accept meaningful ministry in and through the group?

1. Interview singles. Try to find out what their God-given desires are for ministry. Start with the talents that are already in your group and create positions where they can be used.

2. Educate the group about the importance of "every Christian single being a minister." Leaders should constantly encourage the entire group, as well as individuals in the group, concerning their role as ministers, following Jesus' example (Matthew 20:28; John 20:21).

3. Provide opportunities for ministering singles to report how God is working through their ministries. This can encourage other singles to become involved in ministry.

4. Present ministry vacancies as opportunities for service, not as jobs that need to be filled (1 Corinthians 15:58). Keep a positive attitude about the joys involved in serving God. Singles will catch your enthusiasm.

5. Try to discover ministry interests. When you plan council meetings, pass out a blank sheet of paper and have the singles write down the areas of ministry that interest them. Later the leaders should meet and discuss how best to create ministries and ministry teams to fit the desires of individual singles.

6. Provide individual ministry counseling. Spend some time with each single, asking him first what *he* thinks should be done and what *his* vision is for this area of ministry. The important role of the leader should be primarily to help the single work out *his* goals and the steps *he* will take to carry out his ministry. In this way, it becomes God's ministry through the single person.

7. Believe God is working through the singles.

Expect progress, not perfection. Leaders must constantly remind themselves that God has promised to work through the available person. (Read 2 Corinthians 3:5,6.) Instead of taking their ministry away from them when they make mistakes, or doing the work for them, pick them up, help them find out what went wrong, and ask them how they might do it differently in the future. Be an encouragement to them.

Developing Your Planning Council Into a Ministering Team

To expand your singles ministry, you must concentrate on developing your planning council into a ministering team. Increasing numbers in your class meetings or at social functions does not necessarily mean your singles ministry is expanding.

To build a solid and expanding singles ministry, you must develop the talents of your singles. As you do, you will find that your singles ministry will grow both in numbers and in quality.

Planning council meetings are vitally important to the building of relationships among your ministering singles. Time should be given for prayer and worship, and for sharing what God is doing. It is important that the leader share his vision for the group. Other members of the council should be encouraged to share their deepest desires and dreams for the group. It is important to minister to the Lord and to one another, then take care of the group's business.

Here is a suggested schedule for a planning council.

Relationship building. The first scheduled item is fellowship. Our planning council plays together while members are gathering. The activity may be an active sport like volleyball, quiet table games, or friendly conversation.

Sharing times. We usually begin this time by singing worshipful choruses. This leads naturally into the sharing of personal needs, and council members pray for and encourage one another.

Leader's inspiration. The advisor shares the philosophy of the singles ministry and gives guidance as to the purpose of the planning council—why we have come together.

Reports of progress. Different ministry leaders report what is happening in their area of ministry. This is a time of rejoicing as well as a time to determine problem areas and pray about those problems. It is a time of goal setting and establishing a workable plan to achieve those goals. Prayer is a vital part of all the group's activities and is interspersed throughout the planning council.

Nomination of cochairman. It is at this meeting that a new cochairman is nominated. Remember, the previous cochairman assumes the chairmanship of the group, thus vacating the cochairman position. From the list of nominees submitted by the committee members, the executive committee chooses the new cochairman. The person chosen is contacted and asked if he will serve. If so, he and the new chairman are surrounded by planning council members who lay hands on their new leaders and pray that God will anoint them in their ministry.

Sharing by the new chairman. At this point, the new chairman shares his burden, goals, and plans for his upcoming term.

Ministry opportunities. By this time, attenders have caught the spirit of the group, have seen the needs, and are willing to become involved. A sheet of paper with ministry opportunities listed on it is distributed to each person. Each single checks his areas of interest. The executive committee meets later to determine who will be appointed to the ministry positions.

Singles should continually be challenged to look beyond their own group to reach the multitude of singles who are searching. This stage in development is critical because if the singles don't accept the challenge, the life of the group will turn in upon itself and stagnate.

It is amazing how many good ideas can flow forth in a planning council when a spirit of outreach and concern for souls has gripped the hearts of singles. As the group develops a strategy, plans should be laid for integrating newcomers into the group. The Bible calls this integration "hospitality," which literally means "loving strangers." Jesus wants us to take in the stranger: "I was a stranger, and ye took me in" (Matthew 25:35). We prefer to call the visitor a newcomer, and we want him to feel accepted immediately upon coming to the group.

Improving Hospitality and Caring

Here are some suggestions to improve your quality of hospitality.

Make sure you have a "Barnabas" present to welcome every newcomer. Remember, Barnabas was the one who introduced Paul to the Christians in Jerusalem.

Your greeting team must see that newcomers

are given a brief orientation about the group, the schedule, who is going to teach, etc. Then the greeter should introduce the newcomer to a class member who has agreed to sponsor a newcomer for a few weeks. The sponsoring member should introduce the newcomer to other members of the group, sit with him, explain some of the upcoming activities, and offer to take him to an activity. The newcomer should be made to feel he is a part of the group. One of the most important things the sponsor can do is to invite the newcomer to go with him to the next planning council.

Develop a system for caring for regular attenders of the class. We need to be concerned about the singles who have stopped attending. If their needs have not been met, the planning council should discuss ways they can be met better. A caring committee should watch for lax attendance of class members and determine when an absentee needs to be contacted. A single's name should be removed from the roll only when it is discovered that he has moved out of the area, started attending another group, or asked that his name be removed.

Discipling

It is important for singles to pass from one level of involvement to another—participant, planner, minister, discipler. At this fourth level, the single adult commits himself not only to a ministry, but also to helping other singles find their ministry. A discipler places his priority on helping one or more other singles to mature in their relationship with God, with other believers, and with the world.

According to Robert E. Coleman, the discipling process involves the following steps:*

1. Selection—Determine whom you would like to disciple.

2. Association—Spend time with that person.

3. Consecration—Get a commitment from that person that he will learn from you and minister to others under your guidance.

4. Impartation—Teach that person. Share your heartfelt thoughts about your relationship with God, your concerns about ministry, etc.

5. Demonstration—Show him how to minister by having him observe you ministering. Talk it over with him afterward.

6. Delegation—Give him an opportunity to minister—first, while you observe him, then without your presence.

7. Supervision—Keep checking with the person on his progress, what problems he is encountering, etc.

8. Reproduction—Release the person from his discipling relationship with you and encourage him to disciple someone himself.

It is a joy to see a singles ministry, and the individuals who make up that ministry, expand in numbers and, more importantly, in Christian stature. No one can become this deeply involved in a Christian ministry without being stretched in his personal life. Growing people are happy, fulfilled people. That's a major goal and purpose of ministry to singles.

---

*Adapted from Robert E. Coleman, *The Master Plan of Evangelism* [Old Tappan, NJ: Fleming H. Revell Co., 1964], p. 7.

12
The Church and Singles—
Expanding Through
Singles Conferences

"Let's have a singles conference!" said a group of singles in the fall of 1977. "How many would come?" When I suggested that we set a goal of 1,000 in attendance, some laughed—until they realized I was serious. So we went to work planning, praying, working, and getting the word out. About a week before our conference we registered 1,000 people!

We decided, because of the limits of our facilities, to cut off registration at 1,200. We reached that figure 2 days before the conference.

The next year we moved to Seattle Center. The facility there could accommodate up to 3,000 people. The second year we had 1,700 in attendance. Singles came from all over Washington, Oregon, British Columbia, Idaho, and even Hawaii.

Why did they come? They came looking for friendship and an opportunity to meet other singles. "It was valuable for me to be with other singles and to know they face the same problems I do," one single said.

Fellowship opportunities were provided through sharing in small groups, organized fellowship times, and mealtimes. But probably the best fellowship came as singles gathered at the book tables, walked together between seminar sessions, or sat in the fellowship lounge. Another single commented, "I was glad to meet Christian singles who... are finding comfort and trust in the Lord."

They came for help. "I was able to shed a great big load of guilt, condemnation, and fear of the future," a young man said.

Some came bringing their shattered dreams with them. All wanted help to better cope with their lives. One person said, "Attending this conference helped me find new things to praise God for!"

They came to learn. Classes covered a wide area of subjects: prayer, finding God's will, marriage and remarriage, sexuality and intimacy, money management, time management, dealing with emotional needs, and rebuilding a broken life, to name a few. "What I learned here," one single said, "will help me start back into the world I have been hiding from in my hurt."

What began as a dream in the hearts of a few became a reality. But a conference like this does not just happen. We went through four stages in developing and conducting the singles conference.

The Vision Stage

You must see the need for a conference. "Can't we reach singles through our regular programs? Why do we need to go to all the work and effort of putting on a conference?" We felt the conference format was important because it would appeal to a greater number of singles, both Christians and non-Christians. The non-Christians and the uncommitted singles could attend without feeling threatened. We also felt we could use the conference as a tool for outreach in the months preceding it.

You must see the purposes for a conference. Our purposes were fourfold: (1)To show the general public that Christian singles are an energetic, important, wholesome segment of our population, and interested in spiritual things; (2)To provide a Christian context for singles to fellowship; (3)To help meet some of the specific needs of singles—we want singles to become the whole people God intends them to be; and (4)To nurture and build up the Christian singles groups in our area. Some of these groups are small. A conference gives them a chance to be with hundreds of other singles and lets them know they are not alone.

You must see those who can be helped. Try to visualize the various types of singles who will be attending: divorced, widowed, single parents, struggling singles, complacent singles, energetic singles, non-Christian singles.

You must see the end results of a conference. Through eyes of faith you need to see your own singles grow through planning and conducting the conference (Hebrews 11:1). You need to see hundreds of singles being helped and blessed (Proverbs 29:18). You need to see increased attendance in your singles ministry as a result.

The Planning Stage

You must communicate your vision to your singles. It is not enough for you as a leader to have a vision. You must be able to inspire others with the same vision. Nehemiah had a vision to rebuild the walls of Jerusalem. But he couldn't do

to the elderly? Can you see them, like Paul and Silas of old, "turning the world upside down" for Christ? We can, and our hearts rejoice at the vision!

Suppose all of this happened. How would they be supported? Perhaps that opportunity would fall to the Church, to married people too confined by family responsibilities to go themselves. Perhaps that is what this increase in singles is all about. Maybe God wants to use singles as a last effort to see mankind saved before Jesus returns. Maybe they are His power source for the future.

But all these things will never happen unless: first, we reach singles; second, we understand and encourage them in the Christian life; third, we help them develop their talents; and fourth, we send them out with our love, prayers, and financial support to do their work for Jesus.

That's what this book has been about—reaching, teaching, encouraging, accepting, loving, entrusting, and commissioning single people to do God's work. For us it has been a journey of joy. We've stumbled and we've made mistakes as we've worked with single people. But more often than not, they have been the ones to reach down, pick us up, dust us off, and say, "Here's where you went wrong. Next time do it this way." We've listened and learned and grown, and we've become better people because of our association with singles.

"Regardless of all our experiences, the church is still family-centered," says Frank Schneider, director of FOCAS Ministries. "The church must give place to singles. How quickly can the church adjust? I don't know. It almost scares me that the church won't change quickly enough and we'll miss our opportunity."

But suppose we did reach this single generation for Christ. What then? Can you imagine for a moment the strength of this force of people? Can you see them establishing new churches? Can you see them as ministers, missionaries, and part-time lay missionaries in support positions around the world? Think of the strength—the hours—these people could give. Talk to any missionary and he will tell you the great need for secretaries, pressmen, carpenters, technicians of all kinds, electricians, teachers, business managers, nurses, doctors, cooks, and other support people who can carry on the work of Christ on foreign soil. We have the people to meet these needs. We have them *now* in every singles group in this country.

Suppose these singles decided to become a great witnessing force. What if they went out into all the world to preach the gospel? What impact would it make on a world accustomed to thinking of single people as "swingers"? Can you see them talking to migrants in camps around the country, starting Bible studies in singles condominiums and office buildings, witnessing on streets and in missions? Can you see them organizing singles conventions and inviting your city to come hear about Jesus? Can you see them working one-on-one with the sick, the dying, and the imprisoned? Can you see them working with and ministering

fied equally with the married in the communion of the church. (Quoted from Gary Collins, *It's Okay to Be Single* [Waco, TX: Word Books, 1976], p. 51.)

Pastor Charles Anderson says: "We have learned something from our singles groups. They have taught us to be loving, forgiving, and accepting. There is a lot of *agape* love in their groups. That kind of spirit infiltrating the whole church can't help but have a dynamic, positive influence."

The Church Council of Seattle's report on singles states the importance of reaching out to singles this way:

> In reaching out to singles, the church would be committing itself to its own renewal.... The church which consigns singles to the periphery of its vision, or includes them chiefly as objects of pity or judgment, risks being consigned to the periphery of the culture in which it lives. (*Report of the Task Force on the Single Adult in the Church*, Raymond K. Brown, chairperson [Church Council of Greater Seattle and Associated Ministries of Tacoma-Pierce County, April 1977].)

The Potential

Singles are already reshaping our culture and the patterns of life and society. They are affecting the housing industry and consumer goods. They are influencing entertainment. Consider the number of television programs that relate to single women, single fathers, children of divorced parents, and singles in all kinds of living arrangements. Whether you like what you see in these programs or not is beside the point. The point is we are changing this country. We are becoming increasingly "single-minded" and Satan is working hard to corner this market.

ership Among Singles," "How to Attract and Hold Singles," etc.

If it is impossible to attend such a conference, visit a church where there is an active singles ministry. Talk with the leaders, advisors, and pastors in the church. Find out what they are doing, what the pitfalls are, and their goals for the future.

2. *Educate the congregation concerning singles.* This can be accomplished through sermons, teaching, addressing committees and boards, the church bulletin, or newsletters.

Sermons must be geared not just to couples, families, and marriages, but also to singles and single parents. Pastors must believe we are all one in God's eyes, and project that belief to the entire congregation.

3. *Interact with singles.* The pastor himself must be a good friend of singles; visiting the singles groups and getting acquainted with them. He may be a guest teacher for a series. He may attend social events, banquets, retreats, or outdoor events. He needs to let them know he is behind them wholeheartedly.

4. *Give meaningful opportunities to serve within the church.* At the Continental Congress on the Family, Mark W. Lee said:

> We let unmarried women become church secretaries or teachers of small children in Sunday school, and unmarried men become ushers. But why should they not become chairpersons of church boards, development officers, and the like? Singles may engage in Christian occupations and avocations without concern for the needs and comforts of mates.... At the very least, singles should be identi-

You must read about them. Find all the helpful books you can. Read about the widowed experience. Learn what it's like to go through a divorce. Read about single parenting and stepparenting. Learn about blended families and adoptive single parenting. Find out what a handicapped single experiences. Discover why so many people are choosing the single life-style. Devour all the books you can find on the subject.

"Wait a minute," you may say. "I don't have time for that!" We are talking about one-third of the population of this country. In a few years it may be as high as one-half. Doesn't that large a percentage of the population deserve your time and interest? You need to know about this swelling mission field. *You must!*

Talk to singles—not just to groups, but to individuals. Ask them about their needs. Find out what their aspirations are. What would they like the church to do for them? What would they like to do to help the church? Find out if they feel your church is slighting them. See if they feel "second-class."

Attend one of the increasing number of singles conferences that are being held throughout the country. Our church sponsors the Pacific Northwest Christian Singles Convention in March each year. Some of the topics covered at that convention are: "Pressures and Potentials of the Single Life," "Single Parenting," "Coping With Stress," "Divorce—Starting Over," and "Goal Setting."

The church also sponsors singles leadership conferences where topics such as these are thoroughly covered: "How to Begin and Develop Lead-

tians are to be known by their love for each other. This cannot be realized fully if married couples only associate with other married couples, and if singles remain exclusively with singles.

How do we reach out? We reach out by communicating trust through words and actions. We reach out by believing the best about others. It is just as easy to believe the best about someone as it is to imagine the worst.

In plain words, this means that just because a person is single there is not something wrong with him. Sometimes married church members think, "I wonder why he isn't married. There must be something the matter." No, this isn't true. Singleness is a valid life-style. Singles are valued in the eyes of God as much as married people are. He sees us as individuals, single or married, for whom His only Son died. He loves us equally.

We must accept each other in the same way Christ accepts us. We must reach out in faith and love to one another. Because the Church is still largely made up of families and married people, the responsibility for reaching out falls largely on married people. But this does not excuse singles from reaching out too.

Suggestions for Pastors

The pastor is the key person in the integration of singles into the church family. Here are some suggestions for pastors:

1. *Broaden your "single-consciousness."* If you want to know what a certain group is like, you must talk to them. You must ask them questions and *listen* to what they say. You must listen with your ears, but even more with your heart.

Church must reach out to these people. We, the Church, have been flung into a torrent of need!

Reaching Out

We, the Church, need to reach out and draw singles into the fellowship of believers.

When I joined the staff of Calvary Temple, I knew there was an adult singles program in operation, but I gave it little thought. I wasn't against them; I just chose to ignore them. It looked like a great program, but I had no desire to put out time and effort toward singles. It was a nice class that met some people's needs, but at that time I didn't see the potential. Then the church started a second group for younger singles. For the first year another couple sponsored the group, and then I assumed the advisorship. As I became involved with the group, I grew more and more excited about the potential of the ministry.

That is the secret: don't have preconceived ideas about people. Don't label people. We must look on everyone—married, single, young, old, black, white, brown, or yellow—as individuals. James says: "My brothers, as believers in our glorious Lord Jesus Christ, don't show favoritism. ...But if you show favoritism, you sin and are convicted by the law as lawbreakers" (James 2:1,9, *New International Version*).

Couples in a church like to be with other couples. They like to discuss issues relating to marriage. That's all right. It's necessary at times. Singles enjoy being with other singles. That's all right too. But somewhere, sometime, the two groups need to reach out to each other. We all need other people. We can learn from each other. Chris-

13
Single Power

Fifty-two million widowed, divorced, and never-married single people represent a mission field ripe for harvesting. They are potential for the greatest church growth we have ever known. We cannot ignore them. We cannot overlook them. We must reach them now.

Charles Arn, in *The Pastor's Church Growth Handbook,* says:

> A well-tested principle of church growth is that "unchurched people are most responsive to a change in life-style (i.e., becoming Christians and responsible church members) during periods of transition." (Charles Arn, *The Pastor's Church Growth Handbook* [Church Growth Press, 1979], p. 142.)

When individuals are passing through the crisis of a death or divorce, they are most receptive to change. What better change could they make than to commit their lives to Christ?

This theory is born out in fact in our singles groups. Week after week there are large numbers of newcomers. A simple little ad in a community advertising sheet has drawn scores of searching singles. Their need is so great that they come to a group where they know absolutely no one. The

them, and to accompany them to lunch. The way you treat your speakers this year will have a bearing on the speakers you will be able to secure in the future. Word does get around!

If planning has been done well, committee members should be able to enjoy themselves and their work at the conference. Make it a goal that conferees see the conference as well-organized and running smoothly!

The Follow-up Stage

Every attender should be asked to fill out an evaluation at the last general session. These can be collected and sorted by the evaluations committee. Names of participants who say they do not attend a singles group should be given to the follow-up committee. These individuals should be phoned as soon after the conference as possible and invited to your singles group.

Develop a special mailing list of all conference attenders. One to two months after the conference, send out a newsletter featuring highlights of the conference, including pictures, to all conference attenders. List upcoming major singles events, as well as the date of your next singles conference. Whenever you have a major singles event, send these people an announcement.

Schedule some follow-up events, such as a retreat or seminar on some aspect of the single life, and list these on the conference evaluation form. Send information to those who are interested.

The possibilities for follow-up events and ministries are endless. They are only limited by your vision, time, and resources.

follow-up phone call to these agencies can encourage the editors to run the article.

In addition to free forms of advertising, we purchase radio spots coinciding with the time singles drive to and from work. A phone number is given in these spots. We make sure conference staff members are on hand to answer the phone when people call for information.

We have found that the 2 months prior to the conference are the most fruitful period of outreach for our singles ministry. Conference planners have an opportunity to share about the Christian single life with secular professionals whom they contact about the conference. Individual singles can use the brochure as a conversation starter to talk with their friends and business associates about the Christian life-style. A well-planned publicity campaign includes radio and newspaper interviews with Christian singles and conference speakers who share what Christ means to them and how He has made an impact on their lives.

The Event Stage

Greeters and registrars should be in their places as the first conference participants arrive. All conference staff members should be reminded that they are Christ's representatives. They are to greet each person warmly. No one should go away from the conference saying he was not befriended. Counselors must be sensitive to single people in need. They should watch for lonely people and engage them in conversation, showing a Christlike concern for their problems.

Conference speakers should be assigned a host or hostess to guide them to classes, to introduce

have an attractive, professionally designed brochure to advertise your conference. The brochure is the best tool for communicating what you are offering. The design package should include a preliminary flyer ready for distribution 7 to 8 months before the conference, a poster, and a brochure.

You must publicize the conference. Publicize by word of mouth. This is the most effective and least expensive type of publicity.

Use a mailing campaign. We mail conference brochures to everyone on our group's mailing list and to singles on our conference/special events mailing list. This is cheap advertising.

Contact other churches. Send a letter to the pastor with a response card on which he can write the number of brochures and posters he would like to have. State in the letter how the conference can benefit him and his church.

Contact other singles groups. Keep a file of singles groups in your area, listing the name, address, and phone number of their leaders. Some of these groups may bring busloads of singles to your conference.

Distribute posters and brochures. On a specified day, singles from our group who have been assigned areas of the city put up posters in store windows and on bulletin boards in Laundromats, apartment complexes, colleges, and shopping centers. Some merchants will allow you to place quantities of brochures on their counters.

Use public service announcements and news releases. These are free forms of publicity that can reach large segments of the population. Send news releases to community and campus newspapers, and to community organizations. A

name tags, conference packets, conference director's expense, office supplies, refreshments, and publicity. Under income we include registration fees, display booth fees, and tape and book sales.

Second, *the speakers*. Most of your speakers can be qualified local people. If you want cooperation from other churches, it is important to have a good cross section of speakers from many different denominations. Our main purpose in this conference is to meet needs and nurture singles from many different churches and walks of life.

Third, *the schedule*. Remember, singles are working people. Many singles may be driving long distances to get to your conference. Here is a suggested schedule:

> Friday—6:00-7:00 p.m.—Registration
> 7:00-8:15 p.m.—General session
> 8:15-8:30 p.m.—Break
> 8:30-9:30 p.m.—Elective seminars
> 9:30-10:30 p.m.—Fellowship hour
> Saturday—8:00 a.m.—Doors open
> 8:30-9:30 a.m.—General session
> 9:30-9:45 a.m.—Break
> 9:45-10:45 a.m.—Elective seminars
> 10:45-11:00 a.m.—Break
> 11:00-12:00 noon—Elective seminars
> 12:00-1:30 p.m.—Lunch
> 1:30-2:30 p.m.—Elective seminars
> 2:30-2:45 p.m.—Break
> 2:45-3:45 p.m.—Elective seminars
> 3:45-4:00 p.m.—Break
> 4:00-5:00 p.m.—General session
> 7:30 p.m.—Banquet

Fourth, *the brochure*. It is very important to

13 months before—choose date and site of conference. This allows next year's conference to be announced at this year's conference.

11 months before—evaluate past conference.

10 months before—secure keynote speaker; select steering committee; have members fill out preference checklist on areas to oversee; discuss conference schedule, budget, speakers, and theme.

9 months before—give out assignments to steering committee (areas to oversee); explain procedure for enlisting chairmen and coordinators of areas.

7 to 8 months before—secure brochure designer; start contacting speakers; mail preliminary announcement of the conference.

3 to 6 months before—help coordinators and committee chairmen choose committees and workers; work especially hard on publicity.

1 to 2 months before—mail out all brochures; publicity campaign should be in full swing.

1 month before—intense prayer campaign; make sure everything is ready for the conference.

You must build a solid program. There are four areas that can make or break your conference.

First, *the budget.* Try to keep your registration fee as low as possible. We charged a $5 fee at our first singles conference. We set an early registration deadline 1 week prior to the conference. After that date, the fee went up to $10. This will give you a better idea of how many people to expect.

We include the following in our budget: Speakers (honorariums, lodging, meals, and travel), facility expenses, brochures (design, typesetting, printing), postage, confirmation cards, signs,

it alone. Read his rallying cry in Nehemiah 2:17, 18. The writer of the Book of Hebrews admonishes us to spur one another on toward love and good deeds (Hebrews 10:24). The leader with the vision is responsible before God to communicate that vision clearly and forcefully to others.

You must select the right leaders. How important it is to find leaders with the desire and capacity to serve. Leaders for the various committees that plan the conference must be carefully and prayerfully chosen. The first leaders you should select are those who will serve on the conference steering committee. This committee is the nerve center of operations and is the coordinating council for the conference. It sets the budget, determines the schedule, and oversees the work of all committees. Each committee member is given several areas to oversee. In our conferences we have the following areas:

Publicity	Ushers and greeters
Signs	Fellowship activities
Counselors	Elective seminars/facilitators
Convention packet	Information booth
Housing	Taping of speakers
Photography	Equipment & facilities set up
Registration	Telephone answering prior to
Mailings	conference
General sessions	News releases/media coverage
Booths	Letters of appreciation
Evaluations	Speaker entertainment/
Follow up	transportation
Restaurants	Refreshments/catering

You must start planning early. Here is a timetable we use for conference planning: